THE FINANCING OF PUBLIC SCHOOLS IN TENNESSEE

A Guide for the Tennessee Administrator

KEITH D. BREWER, EdD

The Financing of Public Schools in Tennessee

A Guide for the Tennessee Administrator

BY KEITH D. BREWER, EDD

Published by:

LIFEWISE BOOKS

PO BOX 1072

Pinehurst, TX 77362

LifeWiseBooks.com

To contact the author: keithdbrewer.com

ISBN (Print): 978-1-952247-46-0

ISBN (Ebook): 978-1-952247-47-7

DEDICATION

To my wife, Anita, whose love, inspiration and patience encouraged me to write this book. Without her solid support and strength, I would have abandoned the project in its infancy stages. Truly, I am blessed and very fortunate to have such a wonderful person as a mate.

SPECIAL ACKNOWLEDGMENTS

My sincere gratitude is bestowed upon Dr. James W. Whitlock whose expertise proved to be invaluable during my research. Dr. Whitlock was a member of my dissertation committee. His influence has stimulated the inspiration for this book.

A special thanks is given to Wayne Qualls and Bill Emerson for their dedication to providing an equitable education for the students of Tennessee. Their leadership was instrumental in the creation of the Basic Education Program that has provided Tennessee's 141 school districts equitable revenue to educate Tennessee's students.

CONTENTS

PREFACE

The Tennessee school administrator must construct and oversee the school district's budget (director of schools), the school district's budget categories (director of schools and supervisors), and the school's budget (principals). To accomplish these responsibilities, the Tennessee administrator must master the "learning curve" of understanding, building, and administering their first budget. Thus, it is the purpose of this book to serve as a textbook and handbook for the Tennessee administrator.

Chapters 1 and 2 are written to give the reader a contextual background of the history of school finance and to focus on the struggles of states in their attempt to achieve equity and adequacy among its school districts. Both chapters provide a linear view of events and the creation of formulas for the distribution of state revenue to fund public education.

School finance is affected by several interrelated dimensions. The school administrator must be able to define and understand each dimension to broaden the scope of their knowledge of school finance. Chapter 3 explains these interrelated dimensions and conveys the impact that each dimension has upon the school district's budget and budgetary process.

Questions are answered in chapter 4 about the why, how, and need for states and local school districts to utilize federal revenue. This chapter provides details to the past regulations for No Child Left Behind (NCLB) and the current Every Student Succeeds Act (ESSA). Chapter 4 gives an in-depth view of the requirements and regulations that govern special education. To avoid the violation of a student with disabilities rights and account mistakes, Tennessee must possess an awareness and knowledge of federal guidelines and regulations for federal programs.

The Basic Education Program is the distribution formula that is used to fund public education in Tennessee. Tennessee applies this formula in distributing state revenue to its 141 school districts. Chapter 5 is devoted to explaining the formula and provides a copy of the Basic Education Program Manual for the Tennessee administrator in the text of the book.

Chapters 6 and 7 focus on the building and communicating of the district and school budget. These chapters provide a calendar and process to develop a school budget with all stakeholders in a timely manner. Honesty and transparency are exhibited by applying the guidelines given in these chapters.

Chapter 6 provides details for constructing, communicating, and successfully passing a school district's budget. A copy of a typical Tennessee school district's budget is provided on a Tennessee budget document to provide clarity and understanding of the subtleties for a school district budget.

Chapter 7 deals with the school budget. This chapter is particularly informative to the school principal. The primary difference between the school district's budget and the school's budget is that the school principal must utilize the Tennessee Internal School Uniform Accounting Policy Manual to build and to submit his/her budget to the director of schools and school board for approval. The principal must use the manual's accounting methodology and the manual's budget forms. For the principal, the Tennessee Internal School Uniform Accounting Policy Manual becomes the cornerstone for the school's budget.

The sources of funding for Tennessee public education is examined and explained in Chapter 8. Tennessee is somewhat unique in that the state government uses a sales tax to fund its governmental operations. Each county's source of tax is the property tax. Chapter 8 explores these funding resources and discusses the difficulty and complexity of requesting and receiving these funds to operate Tennessee school districts. At the conclusion of chapter 8, I recommend that another source of funding public education in Tennessee needs to be discovered to relieve the burden on the taxpayer for the cost of a quality education.

CHAPTER 1

FINANCING PUBLIC SCHOOLS IN AMERICA

The present concern with equity and adequacy in financing the public schools of America is not new. Rather, this concern reflects the progress made over three-fourths of a century of state and national actions toward achieving adequacy and equity in financing the public schools, actions directed both at equalization of financial resources for children and youth, and equity for taxpayers. During all this time, the great American ideals of equal opportunity including equal educational opportunity have flourished and grown. The social, economic, and political climates that condition application of the "equalization" principle have continuously evolved and changed (Gibbs, 1979).

An understanding of public school requires some basic knowledge of the nature of public schools and how they developed in both their philosophical and historical contexts (Alexander et al., 2015). Therefore, this book will explore the financing of public education in America, examining the different types of distribution formulas of states for dispensing funds to finance public education, the impact of state and federal statutes on school finance, public funding (Peevely, 1980; Brimley and Burrup, 1982), an analysis of equity and adequacy of school finance, financial accounting of school funds, financing school facilities, budget development at the district and school level, financing education with federal funds, and financing public education in Tennessee.

The history of financing public education in the United States is an interesting one. It is fifty separate stories of controversy, of fumbling, false starts, long periods of inaction, and application of various forms and degrees of informal local and state action. In the early part of the nation's history, most of the costs of school operations were defrayed with nonmonetary services provided by school patrons to the school itself or to the teacher. Provision for fuel, custodial services, board and room for teacher, and other similar services were made in lieu of salaries, insurance, and fringe benefits (Brimley and Burrup, 1982).

Although the first mandated school finance activity within this country occurred with the Massachusetts Law of 1647, which required the appointment of teachers and schoolmasters, the state did not provide support for schools. Schools had to be financed at the local level (Peevely, 1980). Many New England colonies used rate bills or tuition, a practice held over from European homelands, to finance education on the local level. Others used the property tax as a method of financing education (Brimley and Burrup, 1982).

It is difficult to determine the exact beginning of state support for public education. Paul Mort reported that by 1890 the existing states provided about $34 million dollars, which amounted to about 24 percent of that year's total school revenue. Since some of that state revenue was obtained from land given to the states by the federal government in the famous Northwest Ordinance of 1787, Mort classified the state funds as state and federal funds (Brimley and Burrup, 1982).

THE FIVE STAGES OF SCHOOL FINANCE

The first of the two stages of development were reflected during the eighteenth and nineteenth centuries. As the first stage of school finance developed and emerged, the local district carried the total financial responsibility for funding education without state assistance. This burden of support eventually became too large for local school districts to finance, and the state's responsibility began to emerge in the nineteenth century. All of the states were utilizing property tax and sending revenue to local districts through flat grants, other forms of grants or aid, and other nonequalizing state allocations.

The twentieth century gave birth to the last three stages of development for school finance. This period of development saw major theorists in the field of school finance come to the forefront with the concepts of the foundation program, refinement of the foundation program concept, and open-ended equalization practices for state governments to dispense money to local districts to yield a high-quality education (Strayer, 1923; Brimley and Burrup, 1982).

EARLY THEORISTS OF SCHOOL FINANCE

Elwood Cubberly (1905) was the first theorist to conceptualize the state's responsibility in apportioning state school funds. Cubberly summarized his philosophy of school finance by stating that all children of the state are equally important and are entitled to have the same advantages. Although Cubberly never believed that this goal would ever be accomplished, his belief hasn't dissuaded parents, students, educators, and school boards from pursuing equity for all children through the court system.

1. Cubberly's tenets serve as a foundation for the framework of school finance today. In 1905, he postulated:

    - Unequal distribution of wealth causes unequal burdens among local school districts.
    - A state tax equalizes these burdens.
    - A state should utilize the average daily membership (ADM) and average daily attendance (ADA) for funding schools.
    - A state should use incentive funds to encourage school districts to provide secondary education, kindergartens, and annual training for teachers.
    - A state should establish a special relief fund for cities and counties that have made the maximum effort

> by law and yet are unable to meet the minimum demands made by the state.

These tenets have been considered or have been adopted in the majority of state distribution formulas of the twenty-first century (Cubberly, 1905).

Harlan Undegraff introduced the idea that general aid granted by the state to local school districts should have a positive relationship to the effort made locally. This effort could be measured by the tax rate. By utilizing this payment-for-effort principle, Undegraff sought to prevent the wasteful use of state aid and to stimulate a greater local interest in schools (Mort, 1933).

George D. Strayer and Robert M. Haig introduced the theory of equalization that introduced the concept of a foundation program. This theoretical conceptualization of equalization postulated that all school districts should receive a minimum educational program (Brimley and Burrup, 1982). Strayer (1923) pointed out that to carry into effect the principle of equalization of educational opportunity and equalization of school support as commonly understood, it would be necessary to (1) establish schools or make other arrangements sufficient to furnish the children in every locality within the state with equal educational opportunities up to some prescribed minimum; and (2) raise the funds necessary for this purpose by local or state taxation adjusted in such manner as to bear upon the state to provide adequately either for the supervision and control of all the schools, or for their direct administration, by a state department of education (p. 173).

Strayer's paradigm centered around nine fundamental factors or standards. First, a foundation program should be devised around the rich district idea—each local district of the state was to provide a foundation, or minimum program. The rich district would receive no state funds; the other districts would receive state funds necessary to provide the foundation program. Second, all foundation programs should guarantee equality of educational opportunity up to a specified point, but all local districts should have the discretionary right to go beyond that point and provide a better program through tax—levy increases. Third, the program would be organized to encourage initiative and efficiency. The other six fundamental factors are prescriptive in that these factors describe how the foundation program should be implemented (Brimley and Burrup, 1982).

The foundation concept did not promote equity or adequacy because the concept only guaranteed the equality of education based on an individual state's definition of a minimum program, and the foundation concept allowed all local school districts in the state to go beyond the minimum to spend for public education. The flawed fundamental factors of the concept allowed wealthier school districts to go beyond the minimum state program and allowed students in wealthier districts to receive more than a minimum or adequate education.

Fast forward to the twenty-first century, the wealthier school districts have thematic academies and comprehensive middle and high schools that offer more than what a state curriculum mandates.

Teachers tend to apply for school districts whose salary and benefits exceed the compensation and benefits of poor school districts. This flaw lowers the quality of teaching in poor districts that is directly reflected in the assessment scores of students. Tennessee was a state that utilized the foundation program to disburse state funds to its school districts. The Tennessee Foundation Program served as an example of a foundation program's factors or standards not providing an equitable education for all students. Tennessee school districts have brought suit against the state of Tennessee on three different occasions over equity and prevailed.

Strayer's conceptual framework did not incorporate a reward of effort or incentive concept in their state support model. On the contrary, Johns et al. (1983) stated that Strayer had attacked these concepts. The foundation concept should not allow any formula to accomplish the double purpose of equalizing resources and rewarding effort due to these elements being mutually inconsistent. Rewards would destroy the very uniformity of effort called for by the doctrine of equality of educational opportunity.

Regardless of deficits, the Strayer concept was a great improvement in the finance of education. It serves as a type of model for most state funding today. However, Brimley and Burrup (1982) still expound upon a central weakness of the concept, when they stated, "School districts of differing financial capacities continue to have unequal abilities to exceed the foundation program. Thus, in the less wealthy districts the foundation program has been not only a 'minimum' but also a near 'maximum' program, for tax levies above the foundation, or base, without state help remit such small amounts of revenue that they discourage local effort to exceed the base program" (p. 142).

Paul Mort did refine the Strayer concept by perfecting amendments to the concept's basic equalization thesis. For example, Mort showed that education costs differ for elementary and secondary pupils. Thus, Mort proclaimed that a unit of need in the foundation plan existed and should be appropriately weighted to reflect these differences (Brimley and Burrup, 1982).

Dr. Gary Peevely (1980) stated that, "Mort was instrumental in popularizing the weighted pupil method of funding schools" (p. 26). "Although Mort's research focused on elementary and secondary schools, his weighted pupil concept was extended to vocational, exceptional, and compensatory educational programs" (Johns et al., 1971, p. 11).

In 1931, Mort directed a national study of state support for education and delivered a eulogy in a synopsis of his survey. His study revealed that in all but a few states, the actual minimum status of education was determined by the economic ability of local districts to support schools rather than the social needs for education. The minimum program in nearly every state was far below the program provided in communities of average wealth. An analysis of the methods used by the different states to measure educational need revealed that no state was using as refined measures as were available. Measures in use were inequitable in one or more of the following respects:

treatment for variation in the size of the school, treatment of districts of the same size, caring for the higher costs of high schools, caring for nonresidents, consideration of costs of living, consideration of transportation, and consideration of capital outlays (Peevely, 1980, p. 27).

Henry C. Morrison was a well-known theorist in the field of instruction and curriculum. Morrison recognized the vast inequalities of wealth among school districts that caused extreme inequalities in educational opportunity. His recognition of these inequalities in educational opportunity would serve as a key point for attorneys representing school districts in the twentieth and twenty-first centuries.

Morrison believed that constitutionally, education was a state function and that local school districts had failed to provide that function efficiently or equitably. His observations had revealed the failure of enlarging school districts, by offering state equalization funds—such as those advocated by Paul Mort—or by offering state subsidies for special purposes. Morrison was critical of the measures that were advocated by Cubberley, Undegraff, Strayer, Haig, and Mort to meet the educational needs of students, and at the same time, providing an equitable system of taxation to support schools. Thus, Morrison proposed full state funding and advocated the use of a state income tax for this purpose.

Today, Hawaii is the only state to adopt a model similar to Morrison's model. Hawaii has established a complete statewide system of education with no local school districts. Although these ideas were not well received by the populist of that day, the defects that Morrison saw in local school financing in the past are still evident today (Johns et al., 1983).

CONCLUSION

Early American education consisted of homeschooling, church-related schools, and private schools. Private schools charged tuition. Poor children were taught reading, writing, spelling, and mathematics by their parents. In the infancy stage of educating children in America, the state did not fund education.

According to Paul Mort, a pioneer in school finance, states finally realized that they had a responsibility to fund education through flat grants, and other nonequalizing state allocations to local school districts. Although a state's participation in funding education was a progressive move for educating children, the problem of equity still existed.

The twentieth century saw the emergence of the Strayer concept of a foundation program. The refinement of this foundation concept created an open-ended equalization practice and stressed high-quality education. Many states, including Tennessee, have utilized the foundation concept to distribute funds to local school districts.

CLASS ACTIVITIES

- In review of the early theorists' concepts, please discuss the concept or combination of concepts that you believe creates an equitable education for all the children in America.
- Select and discuss the theorist that you have determined to have the best concept for the distribution of funds to support education.

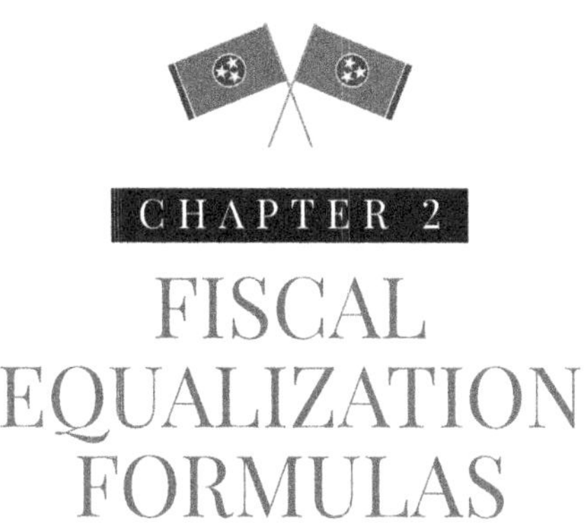

CHAPTER 2

FISCAL EQUALIZATION FORMULAS

The legal authority for the maintenance and operation of public schools has rested with the fifty state governments since the ratification of the Bill of Rights of the United States Constitution in 1791 (Alexander et al., 2015). In most states, local communities and local governments funded the public schools until the original thirteen colonies declared their independence from England and became states. As a result of this transformation from colony to state, each state was required to ratify a state constitution containing a clause that mandated the establishment of public schools. State constitutions were now congruent with the federal constitution and had to offer and fund public education.

Based on the theories of Cubberly, Morrison, Strayer, Haig, and Mort, states have chosen to finance education in three broad categories: Flat grants, equalization grants, and nonequalizing matching grants, but no state uses exactly the same model of state school financing. Historically, changes have constantly occurred in the school finance plans of most states during the general sessions of the legislatures (Johns et al., 1983).

FLAT GRANTS

Early assistance to local school systems came in the form of flat grants. This early method of funding was utilized to provide a form of relief for taxpayers with no real intent of providing equalization (Burrup et al., 1988).

Flat grants may either be uniform or variable grants. The uniform grants are based on per distribution unit and do not consider variation in educational needs nor community financial capacity. Whereas, variable flat grants (i.e., pupil transportation monies) do not consider financial capacity but do compensate for differing classroom or school system needs (Cohn, 1974).

Burrup et al. (1988) conclude that flat grants are generally not equalizing to local school systems, and they confirm that flat grants are still being used in state school finance formulas usually in combination with other equalizing state allocations. Flat grants are commonly used as supplementary categorical aid to the basic or general state school finance program. Such categorical funds are usually used for either pupil-targeted instructional programs or pupil support services (Johns et al., 1983).

EQUALIZATION GRANTS

This model of state funding with allocated funds to local school districts is the reverse proposition to local taxpaying ability. More state funds were given per unit of need to the districts of less wealth than to those of greater wealth. There are two main variations in this equalization model:

1. In computing the cost of the program equalized, a uniform amount is allowed per pupil, per teacher, or per other unit of need, without giving consideration to necessary variations in unit costs of different educational programs and services.
2. Variable amounts per unit of need that take into consideration necessary variations in unit costs are used in computing the cost of the foundation or basic program (Johns et al., 1983, p. 243).

Cohn (1974) divided equalization grants into three types of programs: percentage equalization, guaranteed valuation program, and the Strayer-Haig-Mort foundation program. Since each type of program has merit, most states use a type of the equalizing grant in allocating some or all of their state money to local school districts (Burrup et al., 1988).

The percentage equalizing formula has encouraged the local financial initiative for support of public schools. Each local school district establishes its own expenditures level within state limits, and the state equalizes the expenditures by providing state funds based on the district's relative fiscal capacity. Thus, the level of state funding varied with each school district according to its expenditure level (Johns et al., 1983).

The arithmetic of percentage equalizing is computed as follows (Johns et al., 1983, p. 253):

$$Si = ADM\left(1 - C \times \frac{Vi}{Vs}\right) E$$

Where:

Si = state aid to the *i*th district

C = constant arbitrarily selected having value between 0 and 1.0

Vi = assessed valuation per pupil in the district

Vs = assessed valuation per pupil in state

Ei = educational expenditure level selected in the *i*th district

According to Johns et al. (1983), the dollar level of the local educational program is a function of the local tax effort but not of fiscal capacity. The authors postulate that a poor district with a high level of effort could maintain the same quality educational program as a wealthy school district putting forth the same effort.

The guaranteed valuation approach guarantees a fixed yield from a mandated tax rate. In this type of equalizing program, the state pays the difference between what the tax produces and the guaranteed amount (Cohn, 1974).

The most popular equalization grant is the Strayer-Haig-Mort foundation program. The foundation program concept advocates the idea that all students, regardless of where they live, should be entitled to a quality educational program that is designed to meet their needs (Johns et al., 1983).

The foundation program is very versatile and can be applied with a number of variations. For example, the foundation program concept can be utilized with or without local options to go above the state guaranteed minimum program, with or without state matching of local optional revenues, or in combination with flat grants (Burrup et al., 1988).

The formula that each state uses involves three essential conditions:

- Calculation of the "monetary need" of each school district necessary to obtain a state-guaranteed minimum program, measured objectively in terms of the number of weighted pupils (and other measures of need) to be financed at the level of support that the state will guarantee
- Determination of the amount of local school revenue that can be expected with a state-established uniform tax levied against the equalized assessed valuation of all taxable property within the district
- Determination of the state allocation by finding the difference between the district's established need and the revenue obtainable from its required local tax effort (Burrup et al., 1988, p. 225).

The foundation program formula is computed as follows (Johns et al., 1983, p. 248):

$$Si = Pi\ F - rVi$$

Si = state equalization aid to *i*th district
Pi = pupil ADA, ADM, or FTE weighted for costs of program in *i*th district
F = foundation program dollar value
r = mandated tax rate
Vi = assessed valuation of property of *i*th district

Complications arise in applying the theory in practice for a number of reasons.

- Not all pupils require the same number of dollars of expenditure, even under a commitment to the principle of equality of opportunity. Handicapped children are more expensive to educate than normal ones, and children who attend very small schools and those who attend very large ones are more expensive than those in medium-sized ones.
- Wide variations exist in the assessment practices in the districts of a state, even when all are presumed to be assessed at uniform rates.
- The quality of the teaching staffs may vary considerably, as determined by educational preparation and experience, thus varying the costs of instruction among the districts.

- The dollars provided do not purchase the same amount or quality of goods and services in all districts, thus favoring some districts and penalizing others.
- Some states operate many different kinds of school districts with different taxing responsibilities and restrictions (Burrup et al., 1988, pp. 225–226).

Thus, adjustments have to be made to offset these inequalities. According to Burrup et al. (1988), weightings for school-size differentials, consideration for exceptional children, allowances for transportation, and provision for additional funds for better qualified teachers are the most common adjustments in formulas. State departments and state legislatures have been using four general strategies: (1) full state funding; (2) district reorganization and consolidation; (3) manipulations of general-purpose grant-in-aid systems; and (4) utilization of certain types of categorical grants (Hickrod and Chaudhari, 1972).

CONCLUSION

In reviewing the school funding formulas, one discovers that the Minimum Foundation Program is the most popular. First conceived in the 1930s, the Strayer, Haig, and Mort methodology of funding education has proven to be a sound basis for providing state and local funds to schools in twenty-first century.

Approximately 80 percent of states utilize various forms of the foundation program to allocate state equalization aid to their localities (Alexander et al., 2015, p. 380). The Minimum Foundation Program was never intended to achieve equity among school districts. It was designed to guarantee a base for a minimum educational program throughout a state. School districts were required by their respective state governments to provide funds based upon a uniform local tax effort and were permitted to access additional local funds, if the governmental entities elected to do so (Alexander et al., 2015).

Minimum has been omitted from the Minimum Foundation Program and is now popularly referred to as the Foundation Program. One of the primary characteristics of the Foundation Program formula that made it popular among policy makers is that with limited state resources, coupled with local required tax effort, a specific level of funds was insured throughout the state. An example of a traditional Foundation Program is provided by Alabama, which employs instructional units that are comprised of teachers, principals, counselors, librarians, etc. The instructional units are based upon the number of students per various instructional personnel, and the costs are determined by multiplying the number of instructional units by a series of state-prescribed salaries (Alexander et al., 2015, p. 381).

CLASS ACTIVITIES

- Select a state—Give a written report and PowerPoint presentation to the class that includes the following:
    1. Number of enrolled students in the state's public schools
    2. Amount of the state budget that is appropriated to the public school districts
    3. Name the concept and give the formula that is utilized to distribute revenue to the state's public school districts
- Utilize a concept for distributing revenue for public schools. After the concept selection, create a scenario that you would use to distribute revenue with state funds as commissioner/ superintendent of education for a state. The concept must be equitable and adequate to provide a quality education for all children in your state.
- Define the following terms:
    1. Elwood Cubberly
    2. Foundation Program
    3. Foundation Program Refinement
    4. ADA

5. ADM
6. Categorical Aid
7. Block Grant
8. Flat Grant
9. Budget
10. Budgeted Amounts

CHAPTER 3

INTERRELATED DIMENSIONS OF SCHOOL FINANCE

During the twentieth century, school finance has been impacted and affected by four interrelated dimensions: political, economic, legal, and social. Each dimension has given substance and structure to fiscal policy of states for schools (Sparkman, 1983). The twenty-first century reveals that these same dimensions are still affecting school finance in America.

POLITICAL DIMENSION

In the political dimension, constructing a reform package is a process of active bargaining and partisan mutual adjustment (Brown and Elmore, 1982, p. 121). Policy makers are confronted with a series of trade-offs. For example, each dollar allocated for tax relief is a dollar that cannot be allocated toward equalization of expenditures for school districts (Brown and Elmore, 1982).

Trade-offs are divided into three interdependent packages that correspond to revenues, expenditures, and governance policies. In the revenue area, expenditure trade-offs have to do with the degree to which state support is to be channeled to the local level through unrestricted general aid or through programs that target local expenditures on certain functions or groups.

In similar methodology, expenditures were used to determine the degree to which state support was designed to provide equal rewards for equal effort or simply to reduce expenditure disparities. The expenditure area further determined the degree to which state support was designed to bring low-spending districts up or to hold high-spending districts down (Brown and Elmore, 1982, p. 122).

Governance trade-offs deal with the division of responsibilities between states and localities in tax, expenditure, and program content decisions. Therefore, the basic issue is the degree to which state interests are distinguishable from local interests and the degree to which the former should be translated into explicit controls over local discretion (Brown and Elmore, 1982, p. 122).

"The politics of education in . . . [the 1960s and 1970s] focused on more money, more new programs—and the advocate's task was primarily to demonstrate a need" (McLaughlin and Catterall, 1984, p. 375). The politics of education in the 1980s changed and support for education required different arguments, evidence, and coalitions (McLaughlin and Catterall, 1984).

The decade of the 80s has seen the focus of education politics shift to the states. The following has brought about this shift: accountability, judicial and legislative involvement, increased legislative and general government interest, and new federal education legislation (McLaughlin and Catterall, 1984).

These factors have led many educators to dub their state legislature the "big school board in the sky." Obviously, it doesn't matter what phrase is employed to designate the state legislature's role in education. It seems that teaching is the only profession that legislators dictate by law what to teach, how to teach, and how to evaluate a professional educator through the creation of state statutes. Legislators of states have been thrust into the political arena and will always be a political force in determining school finance policy (McLaughlin and Catterall, 1984).

The state legislature plays the most important role in determining state school fiscal policy (Alexander et al., 2015, p. 139). The legislature must first pass a bill before the governor can either approve or veto it. The legislature deals with school finance matters through a committee structure. The committee structure consists of an education committee in the Senate and House of the legislature, finance committee, ways and means committee, and an appropriations committee in one or both houses.

If an education bill has a price tag attached, the bill may be never be approved in the finance committee to advance to the next committee. Some state finance committees have a preselected amount of revenue that is used to determine the approval of the expenditure. For example, educational programs that exceed $100 million dollars may be more than the committee has agreed to authorize or approve due to state budgetary constraints. As a result, the bill is tabled until the next fiscal year, or bill approval is denied.

ECONOMIC DIMENSION

The economic dimension shapes school finance issues by allocating money and time among competing demands (Sparkman, 1983). Unfortunately, rising costs due to inflation and soaring energy expenses have created serious financial problems for school districts. Local school district decision-makers are having to seek out better ways to allocate limited resources (Geske and Zuelke, 1982).

The economic forecast for public education in the coming decades is quite bleak (Geske and Zuelke, 1982, p. 4). "In the minds of some, education . . . [is] characterized as the great white shark described by the oceanographer in the movie Jaws as an 'eating machine'" (Bedenbaugh, 1985, p. 134). The public perceives education as a devourer of tax revenues. Education in their opinion is constantly consuming money and giving little or nothing in return (Bedenbaugh, 1985).

The condition of the economy has proven to be either a catalyst or depressant to school finance in the past. The greatest advances in equity and expenditures have occurred during periods of high economic growth and relatively low inflation. Likewise, the poorest advances have occurred in times of depression or high inflation (Johns et al., 1983).

This perception has caused the public to demand maximum results for the least amount of money spent. School systems have become accountable to the public. To document this accountability, elaborate cost-effectiveness analyses have been developed. The most frequently used approach to cost-effectiveness has involved this educational production function that expresses mathematically the relationship between school inputs (students, teachers, administrators) and school outputs (growth in cognitive skills, knowledge, and affective behavior (Geske and Zuelke, p. 3). According to a 2019 newspaper article published in Seattle, Washington, the economy still has an effect on American education. "When states cut the budget, they usually cut the discretionary spending first. This often includes money for education and supplemental educational programs" (Education Week, 2019).

Basic problems emerge from within the economic dimension. First, the relationship between cost and the quality of education is difficult to prove because of the complexity of defining and measuring the quality of education. Second, funding the increased cost of education is complicated by the fact that commensurate gains in output cannot be shown for increases in dollar output in education. Finally, the condition of the economy affects not only the first two factors but the total economic dimension depending on its stable or unstable condition.

LEGAL DIMENSION

The legal dimension of school finance has frequently been a catalyst for reform. Over the years, school finance cases have moved away from questions of due process or equal protection to states' responsibilities under their constitutions' articles (Sparkman, 1983). Senator David Dalton of New Jersey remarked that school finance utilization is the important educational issue before the courts and legislature today (Connelly and McGee, 1987, p. 591).

In 1954, the United States Supreme Court for the first time considered the right of the individual as guaranteed in the United States Constitution as having precedence over authority of the individual states to conduct education without question. In Brown v. Board of Education, the United States Supreme Court reasserted that education was a state function and that the federal government could not interfere with state management of education except in cases of practice contrary to federal law. The court ruled that the doctrine of separate but equal facilities was in essence unequal, and therefore, Negro children were deprived of equal protection of the law as guaranteed by the 14th Amendment (Peevely, 1980, p. 32).

A unanimous court recognized that "education is perhaps the most important function of state and local governments... Such an opportunity where the state has undertaken to provide it, is a right which must be made available to all on equal terms" (Brown v. Board of Education).

Brown v. Board of Education set the stage for a new era of thinking as to the availability of certain fundamental rights to all citizens on equal terms. The case was based on two important assumptions: (1) education is perhaps the most important function of state and local government, and (2) it is doubtful that any child may succeed in life if he is denied the opportunity of an education. The decision made it plain that there is no compelling state interest that will justify any racially discriminatory policy in public education.

Almost twenty years after the Brown ruling, the courts were again being asked to consider the proposition that education was a fundamental personal right and protected by the state. The courts were also asked to rule on the system of educational finance, which was thought to be conditioned on the wealth of a child's parents and neighbors, as unlawful. The rising cost of public education, coupled with growing resistance to further property tax increases, and the rising demand for equality in the distribution of public services are two major forces that have brought this issue to the nation's attention through the courts (Peevely, 1980, p. 33).

In practically every state in the nation, wide variations have existed in the amount of taxable wealth available to local school districts. Because their taxing efforts have been limited to the availability of local revenues, the public school systems have been unable to provide equal educational opportunities to their children (Peevely, 1980).

From the few brief references in Brown to various social science studies, school finance came to the point where huge research projects on the effectiveness of schooling, such as the Coleman report, were brought into litigation. In response to the Supreme Court ruling in Brown v. Board of Education, the federal government passed the Civil Rights Act of 1964. The many complex issues raised by Brown caused the Equality of Educational Opportunity Survey of 1966 (known as the Coleman report) to be initiated (Peevely, 1980).

According to Peevely (1980), the first important court case to explore the realm of equal educational opportunity via finance was McInnis v. Shapiro in 1969 in Cook County, Illinois. The suit was filed by a number of elementary and high school students on behalf of themselves and others challenging the constitutionality of various state statues pertaining to the Illinois system of financing their public schools. They sought permanent injunction prohibiting the distribution of tax funds under the laws. The students felt their rights under the 14th Amendment were being violated because state funds were being distributed only on the basis of local assessed valuations and tax rates.

A three-man court ruled that the Illinois program of financing public education reflected rational policy consistent with the mandate of the Illinois Constitution and that there were no constitutional requirements that expenditure be made on the basis of students' educational needs. The court further states that if changes were needed, the change should be pursued through legislation, not through the courts. The case was dismissed, and judgment was later affirmed upon appeal in the case McInnis v. Ogilvie. This decision and the decision by a three-judge federal court in the Virginia case of Burruss v. Wilkerson were to serve as references for similar cases until the case Serrano v. Priest (Peevely, 1980).

On August 30, 1971, the California Supreme Court in the case of Serrano v. Priest handed down a landmark opinion on school finance. Twice, lower courts had dismissed this case before being accepted for review by the California Supreme Court. The court accepted the "fiscal neutrality" approach that argued that the courts should reject existing state financing schemes as arbitrary and unfair. The court's opinion left little doubt as to its ultimate views on the dispute. The court ruled:

> The California public school financing system . . . conditions the full entitlement to (education) on wealth, classified its recipients on the basis of their collective affluence and makes the quality of a child's education depend upon the resources of his school district and ultimately upon the pocketbook of his parents. We find that such financing system as presently constituted is not necessary to the attainment of any compelling state interest. Since it does not withstand the requisite "strict scrutiny", it denies to the plaintiffs and others similarly situated the equal protection of the laws (1971 case of Serrano v. Priest).

The principal features of the court's decision were these:

1. The quality of a child's education cannot be the function of the wealth of the child's parents and neighbors or school district.
2. Education in our public schools is a "fundamental interest" of the states, which cannot be conditioned on wealth.
3. To allot more educational dollars to children of one district than to those of another merely because of the fortuitous presence of commercial and industrial property, which augments a district's tax base, is to make the quality of the child's education dependent upon the location of private commercial and industrial establishments.
4. A funding system that is heavily dependent upon the local property tax and hence the differences of local wealth invidiously discriminates against the poor because it makes the quality of a child's education a function of the wealth of his parents and neighbors. Such discrimination is a violation of the equal protection clause of the 14th Amendment of the United States Constitution.
5. Inequalities are created when people who were relatively less affluent were required to pay higher taxes than the more affluent people in order to generate the financial resources needed for an equal or even lesser quality public education.

It is important to note that there were several positions that the Serrano decision did not take. The courts did not say or suggest:

1. That the property tax, per se, is unconstitutional or an improper tax source
2. That the same amount of money should be spent on each child for education
3. That the legislature must adopt any specific method or plan for school financing to remove the constitutional inequities but would permit the legislatures to devise appropriate new systems, which are not in violation of the equal protection of the law (Education Commission of the States, 1972).

On April 10, 1974, the Superior Court of the State of California for the County of Los Angeles in the case of Serrano v. Priest stated that it was not the function of the court to make a determination of a particular plan for financing public education. The court simply pointed out the objectionable features of the California financing system from an equal-protection-of-the-law standpoint as follows (Peevely, 1980):

1. The basic aid payments of $125 per pupil to the high-wealth school district
2. The rights of voters of each school district to vote tax overrides and raise unlimited revenues at their discretion
3. Disparities between school districts in per pupil expenditures, apart from the categorical aids special

needs program, that do not reduce to insignificant differences, which mean amounts considerably less than $100 per pupil, within a maximum period of six years

4. Variations in tax rates between school districts that are not reduced to nonsubstantial variations within the same maximum period set forth in subparagraph (3) for the equalization of per pupil expenditure levels (Peevely, 1980).

On January 19, 1972 the New Jersey Superior Court of Houston County ruled on Robinson v. Cahill (1972), ordering a revision in the tax structure to remove inequities of the various school districts of New Jersey. On April 3, 1973, the Supreme Court of New Jersey affirmed the judgment of the Superior Court that the current system of school finance in New Jersey was unconstitutional. In doing so, the Supreme Court of New Jersey accepted the lower court's proposition of the relationship between dollars spent and the quality of educational opportunity (Peevely, 1980, p. 37).

There was testimony with respect to the correlation between dollar input per pupil and the end product of the educational process. Obviously, equality of dollar input will not assure equality in educational results. There are individual and group disadvantages, which play a part. Local conditions, too, are telling, for example, insofar as they attract or repel teachers who are free to choose one community rather than another. But it is nonetheless clear that there is a significant connection between the sums expended and the quality of the educational opportunity. And of course, the legislature has acted upon that premise in providing state aid on formulas designed to ameliorate in part the dollar disparities generated by a system of local taxation. Hence, we accept the proposition that the quality of educational opportunity does depend in substantial measure upon the number of dollars invested, notwithstanding that the impact upon students may be unequal because of other factors, natural or environmental (Robinson v. Cahill, 1972).

In 1973, the Supreme Court of the United States determined the constitutionality of state school financing schemes under the Federal Constitution. In San Antonio Independent School District v. Rodriguez, the court ruled that the Texas school finance system did not violate the Equal Protection clause of the 14th Amendment in the Federal Constitution. The court declared that education was not a fundamental right deeming of strict judicial security. Justice Powell stated:

> Education, perhaps even more than welfare assistance, presents a myriad of intractable economic, social, and even philosophical problems. The very complexity of the problems of financing and managing a statewide public school system suggests that there will be more than one constitutionally permissible method of solving them. And that within the limits of rationality, the legislature's efforts to tackle the problems should be entitled to respect (Connelly and McGee, 1987, p. 578).

As a result of the Supreme Court's failure to overturn the Texas program, the states were left with only their own constitution as a basis for challenge. Thus, school financing schemes were challenged in state courts under the state's constitution (Connelly and McGee, 1987, p. 578).

Litigation of the 1980s has seen numerous school finance schemes challenged in our judicial system. The following selected cases have been affirmed as constitutional:

1. **McDaniel v. Thomas**—Plaintiff parents, children, and school officials brought suit against the state authorities claiming that the existing public school financing scheme of Georgia violated the state's equal protection provisions and deprived children of an adequate education. The trial court agreed with the plaintiffs' contention that the system of financing public education violated the state's equal protection provision but rejected the plaintiffs' arguments regarding an adequate education. The Georgia Supreme Court later reversed the lower court's opinion on the state's equal protection provision.

2. **Lujan v. Colorado State Board of Education**—The appellee were school children residing in 16 of the 181 school districts within the state who, as plaintiffs, claimed that the state finance system was unconstitutional. The Supreme Court of Colorado reversed a district's court ruling and found that the Colorado state system of financing public elementary

and secondary education was constitutionally permissible.

3. **Board of Education v. Levittown, etc. v. Nyquist**—In this 1982 case, the New York Court of Appeals overturned two lower court's decision by upholding the state's financing system. The court addressed the issue by stating that existing inequalities were the product of demographic, economic, and political factors intrinsic to the cities themselves and were not attributable to legislative action or inaction.

4. **Hornbeck v. Somerset County Board of Education**—The court held that the thorough and efficient clause of the Maryland Constitution did not mandate exact equality of per pupil funding and expenditures among the school districts.

5. **Horton v. Meskill**—The Connecticut Supreme Court held that the state financing scheme was constitutional. In addition, the court held that the state categorical grant program for financing transportation, special education, and school construction were constitutional (Connelly and McGee, 1987, pp. 578–582).

The following cases were declared unconstitutional:

1. **Washakie County School District No. One v. Herschel**—The appellants, three school districts, the school board members of these districts, and several

students who attended schools in Washakie County brought suit challenging the Wyoming State financing scheme as violative of the equal education provision of the Wyoming Constitution. The Supreme Court held that the state's system of financing public education was unconstitutional in that it failed to afford equal protection in violation of the state's constitutional mandate. The court concluded that until equality of financing is achieved, there is not a practicable method of achieving equality of quality.

2. **Dupree v. Alma School District No. 30 of Crawford County**—The Arkansas Supreme Court held that "property poor" school districts and the students therein were denied the equal protection of the Arkansas state constitution. The court's opinion was that no rational relationship could be found to exist between the financing system, which was based largely on the local property tax base of the school districts, and the educational needs of the districts (Connelly and McGee, 1987, pp. 582–583).

Connelly and McGee (1987, p. 591) have provided the following summary of school of school finance litigation in the 80s:

1. Property wealth was an issue in ten of the court cases.
2. Five of these decisions upheld their state scheme.
3. Two of these decisions did not uphold their state scheme.

4. Two are awaiting final decisions.
5. The current trend seems to favor upholding state finance schemes.

Legal challenges attacking the finance formulas of states have currently slowed down from the rapid pace of the past. For example, in the 1980s twelve states had lawsuits pending, and at least five states had legal challenges planned. However, the litigated issues (equity and adequacy) remain the same today. To illustrate this point, the following is a summary of those states with pending and prospective school finance litigation in the twentieth century (Newman, 1990).

Alaska—Several districts located within cities and towns were suing the state for more funding. Schools in unincorporated areas received more state aid than did those in cities or towns. According to the spokesman for the education department, the state provided more funding to unincorporated districts because they did not have local government to levy taxes.

Connecticut—A year-old suit argued that the state did not provide equal educational opportunity as guaranteed by the state constitution. The plaintiffs' brief alleged that urban school children were being denied "equal educational opportunity" because they had poor-quality schools, and suburban students were denied the opportunity to "associate with and learn from" the minority students in the cities.

Indiana—The original suit was filed in 1987 by the Lake Central school district. More than fifty-one districts are now plaintiffs in the suit, according to Thomas Roman, Superintendent of Lake Central Schools.

Massachusetts—This case involved a constitutional issue and had begun at the level of the state supreme court. The state constitution required only that the legislature "cherish the interests of literature and the sciences." The Massachusetts Teachers Association had begun a campaign to have that language changed to ensure "equal educational opportunity" for all children without regard to residence.

Michigan—More than 120 school districts were suing the state to remove a "procedural roadblock" to a school finance suit.

Minnesota—The suit Skeen v. Minnesota. alleged that the state's funding formula discriminated against poor districts. Their argument focused on the so-called local option tax, which they said was illegal because wealthy localities raise more money with it than poor districts did.

North Dakota—The North Dakota constitution required the legislature provide for a "free and uniform" education. Nine school districts and several dozen parents and students were plaintiffs in the suit.

Oregon—Although their case was dismissed earlier by a county judge, plaintiffs challenging the school funding formula said they will continue their litigation. The state supreme court ruled in 1976 that the funding formula was constitutional, and the judge dismissed the current suit on that basis.

Alabama—Fourteen districts have filed a school finance lawsuit.

Illinois—A school finance lawsuit "is very likely" within the next year. About twenty districts had joined a coalition seeking to change the state's school funding formula.

Pennsylvania—About thirty school boards "had given approval or had expressed an interest" in filing a suit.

Virginia—Several superintendents were contemplating legal action.

Wyoming—A group of three districts were seeking to change the state's school funding formula.

SOCIAL DIMENSION

The fourth interrelated dimension of school finance is the social dimension. Public schools operate and are subject to the many pressures that emerge in a social context (Sparkman, 1983, p. 300). Society, throughout history, has caused change in education.

In 1983, Allan Odden predicted that three major social trends would add new issues to the school finance policy agenda in the future. According to Odden, the political context for education funding has changed. The improvement of education has become instrumentally linked to the key domestic issues facing the nation and each state. (Odden, 1983)

The increased number of people employed with long-term jobs and the increased economic growth in a state definitely provides more revenue for state and local governments to spend on education. Most states now have realistic budgets and are able to create adequate "rainy day" funds. Federal reforms in education have increased the awareness of the necessity of quality education, and state legislatures have created accountability systems that ensure the quality of education. The most recent federal legislation (Every Student Succeeds Act) is a primary example of spending federal and state dollars that focuses and ensures the quality of education.

CONCLUSION

The political, economic, legal, and social dimensions are the keys to the funding of an equitable and adequate education for all students. It seems these four dimensions have more negatives than positives in educating all students in the twenty-first century.

The political dimension attempts to capture the dynamic tension involved in making public policy when policy makers are confronted with the difficult choice of allocating scarce fiscal resources across multiple objectives (Sparkman, 1983).

Interest groups usually formulate those objectives. Over the years, this interest group participation has broadened to include, not only educators, but also business and tax relief advocates (Brown and Elmore, 1982). School finance has become contingent on business, agriculture, and taxpayer groups being amply represented and involved in the construction of the reform, in addition to educational interests.

Today the economic forecast for America is precarious. America is either worried about an inflation or a depression.

The Federal Reserve is lowering the prime rate of interest, or businesses are reducing their workforce.

A cloudy forecast on the economy of America has a negative impact on education. The America taxpayer has several priorities that come before increasing the revenue to improve teacher compensation, fund new classroom construction, and supply all students in America with advanced instructional technology and equipment. However, the populace will always pay for roads, jails, police cars, fire engines, and medical protection before education.

CLASS ACTIVITIES

- Explain the four interrelated dimensions that affect school finance.
- Has the political, economic, legal, and social dimensions shaped school finance in Tennessee? Why? Why not?
- Research the following case, San Antonio Independent School District v. Rodriguez, 411 U.S. 1 (1973) and give a narrative review by utilizing the following format:
    - Facts—What is the topic of the case being litigated?

- Holding—What was the decision rendered in the case?
- Basis—What was the nexus of law used by the court in rendering a decision?

CHAPTER 4

FINANCING PUBLIC EDUCATION WITH FEDERAL REVENUE

If public education is the state's responsibility, why is the federal government involved in assisting each state with federal revenue? Do states and school districts really need federal dollars to educate children in America? Why do we have regulations tied to the federal revenue that each state receives? These are legitimate questions that each administrator and educator have asked themselves during their career. Most educators are never able to find the time to discover the answers or really cared to find the answers. After all, the children and educational practitioners are benefiting from federal dollars by closing the student achievement gap or by having a job and utilizing the supplies and equipment through revenue supplied by the federal government.

Alexander et al. (2015) acknowledged, "The role of the federal government in the financing of American education has historically been a subject of considerable controversy. Many believe that the federal government has a special responsibility for education that emanates from a national interest in the general welfare of America, and that this responsibility requires substantial federal financial commitment. Others maintain that the nature of American federalism places little financial reasonability of education on the central government. Others cling to the point of view that the federal government should give money to serve as a stimulus for change and innovation or to deal with educational needs that are of particular national interest. Some citizenry believe that the federal government should only give federal aid to enhance competition among school districts, schools, parents and students" (p. 208).

Why is the Federal Government Involved in Assisting Each State with Federal Revenue?

The General Welfare Clause of Article I, Section 8 (Constitution of the United States), provides, "The Congress shall have power to lay and collect taxes, duties, imposts and excises, to pay the debts and provide for the common defense and general welfare of the Unites States." Alexander Hamilton maintained that this article conferred upon the Congress the substantive power to tax and spend for the general welfare of the United States. The General Welfare Clause gave Congress a qualified authority in education.

The combination of the General Welfare Clause and the 10th Amendment prescribe to Congress the power to spend for education. States are induced to take federal money but are not mandated to obtain federal money. If federal revenue is requested and obtained by a state, the state's education system must comply with the rules and regulations that governs the use of the revenue for spending. The Supreme Court has affirmed in the cases of *Rowley* and *Arlington* (special education cases) that when a state applies and obtains revenue from the federal government, a contract now exists. The contract between Congress and the state yields the amount of money that the state receives and the rules and regulations that the state must comply to spend the federal dollars (Alexander et al., 2015).

Do States and School Districts Really Need Federal Dollars to Educate Children in America?

A state would be unable to yield a quality education for its children without federal assistance. The tax burden would be of such magnitude that the residents of the state would not be able to pay the cost for educating the children that reside in the state's borders. For example, the state of Tennessee does not have a state income tax for Tennesseans. Tennessee relies primarily on the sales tax levied for clothes, cars, and food, and the counties rely on their property tax and a portion of the sales tax to fund education.

Tennessee's sales tax is 9.75 percent in almost every county. The county, city, and the state divide this rate to fund state and county services. Education receives a portion of the sales tax and property tax. Without federal assistance, Tennessee would need to create another revenue source (state income tax), and local governmental entities would need to raise property tax and create another source of tax revenue (wheel tax). A poor southern state would become poorer, and an adequate education becomes an inadequate education for Tennessee's children.

States and school districts need federal dollars to educate children. Without federal funding, student achievement, the quality educators, and the general welfare of the populous would be at risk.

When Did the Federal Government Become Involved in Providing Federal Aid to Education?

Even though there is no complete record of all the federal funds that are, or have been, expended for education, one is able to determine the historical development of federal aid. For example, Congress, operating under the Articles of Confederation, set aside lands from the national domain for public schools in each new state upon entry into the Union.

The Articles of Confederation utilized ordinances to provide federal aid. The Ordinance of 1785 specified a portion of land in each state for the creation of public schools, and the Ordinance of 1787 enunciated the belief that education was necessary for good government and the happiness of the people. The Ordinances of 1785 and 1787 became the genesis of the federal government's involvement in the financing of public schools in the United States without exercising any control over education as a condition for receiving these land grants.

According to Kern Alexander (Alexander et al., 2015, p. 227), one of the most potent forces in the establishment and financing of public schools in the United States was the federal land-grant policy. The Morrill Act was passed by Congress in1862 providing a grant of 30,000 acres to each state for each representative and senator in Congress. The Morrill Act extended the same right for states that were admitted to the Union after 1862. For states that had insufficient public lands to make up the allotment, a certificate was provided to sell the land, and the proceeds were used for the

> .... endowment, maintenance and support of a least one college where the leading object shall be with excluding other scientific and classical studies and including military tactics, to teach such branches of learning as are related to agriculture and mechanic arts in such manner as the legislatures of the state may respectively prescribe (Alexander et al., 2015, p. 227).

The federal government became more involved in the twentieth century. In 1914 and 1917, Congress passed the Smith-Lever Act and the Smith-Hughes Act. Both of these acts were more specific in detailing the purposes for which the grant funds could be spent. For example, the federal revenue for the Smith-Lever Act provided money for extension services by county agricultural agents, home demonstration agents, and training for teachers in those subject areas, and the Smith-Hughes Act provided vocational funds below the college level to vocational agriculture, trades and industry, and homemaking. The Smith-Hughes Act provided the first special-purpose grants to public schools by Congress.

A major federal initiative for vocational education took place when Congress enacted the Vocational Education Act of 1963—Public Law 88-210 (Alexander et al., 2015, p. 229). This law quadrupled the federal appropriations for vocational education. Federal dollars were purposed to improve the quality and achievement level of programs that did not require a baccalaureate degree. The law further provided assistance for construction of area vocational facilities, work-study programs, and residential schools.

In the twenty-first century, the reauthorization of the Carl D. Perkins Career and Technical Education Act of 2006 (CTE) gave an increased focus on academic achievement in career and technical education by enhancing the connections between secondary and postsecondary education (Alexander et al., 2015). The Carl D. Perkins Act of 2006 officially changed the unit name from Vocational Education to Career and Technical Education (CTE) for high school occupational training.

Why Do Public Schools Have Regulations Tied to Federal Revenue That Each State Receives?

Revenue that is distributed by the federal government to states for public education is directed revenue. Federal revenue is focused on students in poverty, minorities, students with limited English language skills, and students with disabilities. Rules and regulations ensure that federal revenue is expended on these subgroups. According to Dr. Stephen Wright, former

Elementary and Secondary Education Act (ESEA) director for Knox County Schools, federal regulations are a necessity to channel funds to the disadvantaged student. Without federal regulations, the student achievement gap that exists among these subgroups would minimally be reduced (Wright, 2020).

How Is Elementary and Secondary Education Act of 1965 (ESEA) and the Individuals with Disabilities Education Act (IDEA) Funded?

In terms of funding, two of the most important federal education acts are ESEA and IDEA (Alexander et al., 2015). Along with the additional revenue from Congress came more federal regulations. In fact, the creation and passage of these acts have ensured that federal intrusion, both monetarily and regulatory, have solidified the education partnership between the federal government and state governments.

Even though it is optional for a state to accept federal dollars. Every state has accepted ESEA and IDEA money and will continue to accept these funds in the future. If states did not receive federal assistance, public schools would never be able to meet the growing curriculum that students today and students of the future must master to compete in a global economy. The downside of accepting federal funding is the regulations that states must comply with and the amount of paperwork for state and local school districts must complete for accessibility to the federal revenue.

More paperwork was required under ESEA because the act had a number of categorical programs. The numerous categorical programs became a burden on states and school districts due to the extensive reporting requirements. To minimize these reporting requirements, Congress has passed the Education Consolidation and Improvement Act (ECIA), which became effective in July 1982. This act has consolidated funding sources and the accompanying procedures and processes (Alexander et al. 2015). Under the new act, several categorical programs are replaced by block grants, and the block grant consolidation is designated and defined in two chapters (Alexander and Salmon, 1995).

Chapter 1, Title I, ESEA. This part has authorized the continuation of Title I, ESEA and rewrote several administrative provisions to reduce reporting requirements (Alexander and Salmon, 1995, p. 289). Chapter I funds are allocated in two basic types of grants: basic and concentration.

Approximately 89 percent of Chapter 1 funds in 1992 are basic grants. Basic grants are allocated annually to counties according to a formula that uses two factors: the number of formula-eligible children in each county and the average expenditure per pupil (Alexander and Salmon, 1995, p. 289).

Concentration grants allocate supplemental funds to local educational agencies with a high percentage of poor children. If the number of poor children exceed 6,500 or the number of poor children constitutes 15 percent or more of all school-age children (ages 5–17) in the county, the school district will receive an allocation of funds determined by a formula stipulated by the grant (Alexander and Salmon, 1995).

Chapter 2, Title I, ESEA. The purpose of Chapter 2 is to enable state and local educational agencies to implement promising or innovative programs that can be demonstrated to be effective in improving student achievement, student behavior, teaching, learning, and school management (Alexander and Salmon, 1995).

The ESEA was reauthorized in 2001, and a new acronym was given to the reauthorized act. Henceforth, the Elementary and Secondary Education Act (ESEA) would be known as the No Child Left Behind (NCLB) Act. NCLB was proposed by President George W. Bush and was signed into law on January 8, 2001. Features of the law called for states to institute standards-based reform and high student achievement standards with measurable goals for students that could be assessed and evaluated (Alexander et al., 2015).

The NCLB did not provide a national achievement standard, but the law did require each individual state to set its own achievement standard. Thus, the Adequate Yearly Progress (AYP) toward meeting the state standard was assessed by each state's annual test scores (Alexander et al. 2015).

The most important elements of the new law were the penalties to be imposed on public schools and school districts. The penalties were prescribed and mandated in law. In accordance with the law failure for a school to achieve the AYP toward the standard mandated a restructuring process by the fourth year and continuing until the sixth consecutive that required the school to be closed, granting a charter for the school to a chartering agency, or have the school run directly by the state education agency.

NCLB became a troublesome law for most of the states. States had stress in getting federal approval for their applications to receive federal funds. The penalties were stressful for students, teachers, and administrators. In Tennessee, the teacher, principal, superintendent, and school board organizations were united in their opposition to the NCLB Act. However, federal revenue has increased more than five billion dollars or 56 percent since the passage of NCLB (Alexander et al., 2015, p. 233), and this increased revenue could not be turned down by Tennessee or any other state.

On December 10, 2015, the Every Student Succeeds ACT (ESSA) was signed by President Obama. This bipartisan legislation reauthorizes the fifty-year-old ESEA and replaced the NCLB Act. ESSA is the nation's main education law for all public schools in America.

ESSA had the same purpose as the NCLB Act. Both acts were signed into federal law to make sure that public schools provide a quality education for all students in public schools. According to Andrew Lee, ESSA gives states more authority in how schools account for student achievement. Disadvantaged students are included and placed into four groups:

- Students in poverty
- Minorities
- Students with disabilities special education

- Students with limited English language skills

Under ESSA, states get to decide the education plans for their schools with a framework provided by the federal government. Each state must provide the federal government a plan for addressing the needs for all students. For example, students with disabilities must have a plan to meet their needs. The parents are involved in developing this plan with their child's teacher or teachers. The Individualized Educational Plan (IEP) becomes a contract between the school and parents to ensure their child's needs are met. Similarly, regular education students and the other groups of disadvantaged students all have plans that must address the following areas (US Department of Education, 2015):

- Academic standards
- Annual testing
- School accountability
- Goals for academic achievement
- Plans for supporting and improving struggling schools
- State and local report cards

ACADEMIC STANDARDS

ESSA allows each state to set its own general education standards and coursework for schools. The education standards are set for each grade level. The academic standards should be challenging for all students (including those with learning and thinking differences) in reading, mathematics, and science to enable students to succeed in college or in a career (ESSA, 2015).

ANNUAL TESTING

States must test students (3–8 and high school) in reading, math, and science once a year. States must provide accommodations on these assessments and list them in the students' IEPs or 504 plans.

One percent of students with cognitive disabilities can be given alternate assessments that are assessments different from the state's general education assessments (ESSA, 2015).

SCHOOL ACCOUNTABILITY

A state must choose a minimum of five ways to measure school performance. The first four are academic indicators and are mandatory. The plan must show how the school and school district are doing on academic achievement, academic progress, English language proficiency, and high school graduation rates.

The fifth measure must be a way to measure school quality or student success. A state can select more than one method to accomplish this ESSA requirement. Thus, states have the opportunity to choose kindergarten readiness, access to and completion of advanced course work, college readiness, discipline rates, and chronic absenteeism (ESSA, 2015).

GOALS FOR ACADEMIC ACHIEVEMENT

In accordance with the federal law (ESSA, 2015), states must set achievement goals for students. A state must demonstrate if students are improving or not improving. The federal statute is very specific that states must validate academic improvement with all students, especially the students with disabilities, students in poverty, minorities, and students with limited English language skills.

PLANS FOR IMPROVING STRUGGLING SCHOOLS

ESSA requires that states identify struggling schools and place the schools into two categories. The lowest performing schools will be classified in the category of Comprehensive Support and Improvement, and schools where certain student groups are consistently underperforming will be classified in the category of Targeted Support and Improvement.

If a school is recognized as being in either of these two categories, the state and school district must create a plan to assist in improving the struggling school. In collaboration with the parents, the law requires that the plans must use evidence-based teaching and evidence-based programs. ESSA requires that if a state identifies a school or subgroup as struggling, the parents must be notified (ESSA, 2015).

STATE AND LOCAL REPORT CARDS

The law (ESSA, 2015) requires that each state and school district publish report cards. The state and school district report card should display test score results, high school graduation rates, school funding information, teacher qualifications, and details on subgroups of students (minority students, students in poverty, limited English language skills, and students with disabilities).

THE ROLE PARENTS PLAY IN ESSA

ESSA requires states to let parents get involved in the accountability process for schools. Their input will help ensure that schools pay attention to students with disabilities. To enhance the role of parents, ESSA dictates that parents should be included in formulating goals for achievement, accountability, and struggling students for state and local plans. ESSA further emphasizes the role of parents by requiring the involvement of parents in the development of state and school district report card information to inform the public how schools are doing (ESSA, 2015).

INDIVIDUALS WITH DISABILITIES EDUCATION ACT (IDEA)

The other source of federal revenue that states utilize comes from the IDEA. Similar to the original ESEA, this federal revenue is essential for states and school districts to provide a free education for all students. Without these federal revenue sources, the burden of meeting all the students' educational needs would be impossible for states and school districts to achieve.

IDEA became a law in 1975 and required states to provide children with special education services as a condition of receiving federal funds. IDEA has mandated that schools provide a free appropriate public education. In order for states to meet their responsibility of providing a free an appropriate public education, states must apply for revenue to meet the disabled child's needs and accept the regulations that the law stipulates (Hancock, 2019).

Any state seeking to obtain funds pursuant to the IDEA must submit a state plan to the United States Secretary of Education. The plan must provide assurances that show, among other things, that the state has a policy ensuring that all IDEA eligible children have the right to a free appropriate public education (Norlin, 2009).

An approved plan for IDEA funding does not cover all the funding necessary for serving students with disabilities. The state and school districts are responsible for the funding residual that the federal revenue does not cover. IDEA funding is not intended to shift the obligation from the states to the federal government. IDEA funding may be described as being assistive in meeting the excess costs of educating a student with a disability (Norlin, 2009).

IDEA funds are distributed through three main grant programs and several competitive categorical or discretionary programs. Part B of IDEA is the main and largest program in the law and provides funds to state and local agencies to offset the excess costs of educating disabled children. Part B funding has two basic parts (Alexander et al., 2015):

1. A provision that guarantees base funding will not be less than the amount appropriated during the 1999 fiscal year.
2. A provision that provides funds above the 1999 level will be distributed at a level above the previous year with 85 percent allocated to states as determined by the state's share of children within the law's age range (3 to 21 years), and 15 percent is allocated based on the state's share of children within the law's age range that are living in poverty.

Part B funding also provides for state administrative costs of up to 10 percent of the grant for other state-level activities, such as monitoring, professional development, and establishing risk pools. The law provides for a maximum of $800,000 or the state's set-aside for administration of the FY 2004 base year (Alexander et al., 2015).

IDEA proposed that federal funds should cover up to 40 percent of the excess cost of educating students with disabilities. IDEA celebrated its 45th anniversary in 2020, and the act had not reached that 40 percent of maximum. In FY2011, the federal government appropriated $11.5 billion or 16.1 percent of IDEA to cover the costs of students with disabilities, and IDEA contributed $25,069,721,000 or 30.6 percent of revenue for students with disabilities. Gradually, it seems that the federal government will fulfil the 1975 law by fully funding IDEA by FY2021 ($35,308,178,000 or 40 percent). As a result of this landmark legislation, today (Ellerson, 2019):

- Over 6.6 million students receive special education services designed to meet their needs.
- 95 percent of students with disabilities attend a neighborhood school, of which 60 percent spend at least 80 percent of their day within the regular school environment.
- Nearly 350,000 infants and toddlers receive early intervention services.
- Almost six out of ten students with disabilities graduate high school with a regular diploma—twice the percentage of twenty-five years ago.
- Approximately half of the students with disabilities enroll in postsecondary education.

IDEA has a nonsupplanting requirement that prevents states and local school districts utilizing federal IDEA funding to relieve them of their obligations to finance the education of students with disabilities. To prevent that, the federal government requires that IDEA funding be used to supplement and increase the level of state and local funds spent on educating students with disabilities and never to supplant those expenditures. The IDEA regulations contain a state level and local level nonsupplanting requirement (Norlin, 2009).

Likewise, IDEA also imposes a maintenance of effort requirement as part of the local level nonsupplanting requirement. Maintenance of effort requires that in any particular fiscal year each district must spend the same amount of state and local funds on special education as it did in the previous year, either on an aggregate or per capital basis. However, the law identifies special circumstances when a school district may reduce its special education outlay during a particular year. These exceptional circumstances are (Norlin, 2009):

- The voluntary departure, by retirement or otherwise, or departure for just cause, of special education personnel who are paid at or near the top of the agency salary scale
- A decrease in the enrollment of children with disabilities
- The end of the Local Education Agency's responsibility to provide an exceptionally costly program to a child with a disability because the child has left the agency's jurisdiction, no longer requires such a program, or has aged-out with respect to the agency's responsibility
- The end of costly large expenditures for long-term purchases, such as equipment and construction

CONCLUSION

Federal revenue for America's public schools is a necessity. Without federal funds for public schools, Tennessee's public school achievement levels would decline, and the tax burden on the city and county schools would be troublesome for wealthy school districts and overwhelming for poor school districts. As a result, Tennessee school districts would be in chaos.

A former Tennessee special education director reports that educating students with disabilities in her school district without federal revenue would be an unrealistic goal. (Brewer, 2020) According to *Education Week* (2019), the federal funding for special education across the United States for students with disabilities has increased to 23 percent. With each reauthorization or amending of the IDEA, one sees an increase in federal funding. The federal government is striving to reach a 30-percent level of funding with the passage of the Individuals with Disabilities Education Improvement Act (IDEIA).

It is obvious that states cannot educate students with disabilities without federal funding. Superintendents, boards of education, and principals may complain about the rules and regulations associated with their acceptance of federal funding, but without the federal government's assistance, the student achievement gap among students in poverty, students with disabilities, minority students, and students with limited English language skills would not be reduced. School districts would not be able to meet federal and state accountability mandates. Local property tax would increase, and the collection rate would decrease. The teaching and learning environment would be in a state of confusion and disarray.

CLASS ACTIVITIES

- Interview a Tennessee special education director/ supervisor from a rural or urban school district.
- Interview a Tennessee federal projects director/ supervisor from a rural or urban school district.
- What changes would you make to the ESSA?
- What sources of local revenue do school districts in Tennessee utilize to fund education?

CHAPTER 5

FINANCING TENNESSEE EDUCATION WITH THE BASIC EDUCATION PROGRAM

Schools cannot operate without money. The revenue for operating public schools in America come from three primary sources:

1. Federal government
2. State government
3. Local government

State and local governments provide school funding from several resources that vary from state to state and school district to school district. States use a combination of income tax, corporate tax, sales tax, and fees to provide about 48 percent of the budget for elementary and secondary schools. Local governments contribute around 44 percent, drawn mostly from local property taxes, and the federal government gives approximately 8 percent of state education budgets (National Center for Education Statistics, 2010). Altogether, these funds are distributed to school districts on a per-pupil basis to ensure there is enough to cover each child's education (Education Week, 2007).

Every state has its own formula and system for financing education. It is the responsibility of the state to create and implement a funding formula that provides equity and adequacy for students and teachers. Wherever a student resides in the state, he/she should receive a free and appropriate education that meets academic expectations. Likewise, a teacher should receive the same rights and pay that are equitable with other teachers in the state. Unfortunately, states often fail at providing equity and adequacy to students and teachers.

Daarel Burnette stated, "More than a third of the nation's states distribute billions of K–12 dollars in a regressive manner, spending more on wealthier students than on impoverished students according to a new report by the Education Law Center, and advocacy organization focused on fiscal equity in public education. Seventeen states spend an equal amount of money between wealthy and poor students, even though research show poor students are more expensive to educate" (Burnette, 2019).

In its annual "Making the Grade" report release in 2019, the blame is placed on aging state funding formulas and increasing property rates among children for district budget cuts, stagnant teacher pay, and academic achievement gaps

(Education Week, 2019). The report was very incriminating for Mississippi, Tennessee, and Texas. All three of these states receive low marks for spending more money on wealthy districts than poor districts.

It is not an easy or simple task to create a funding formula that is both equitable and adequate. A funding formula that was adequate and equitable a decade ago may not be today. Due to a change in student population and a state's economy, every state's funding formula needs to be reviewed and modified to meet the challenges that have been created over the passage of time. If a state ignores the monitoring of their funding formula or not heeding the advice of their oversight committee, a lawsuit usually occurs.

Court battles have repeatedly determined that states are responsible for all education spending and that even when their funding is simply a minor supplement to local budgets, states should not allow one district to spend vastly more than another (Education Week, 2019).

A wave of litigation occurred in the 1980s. The litigants focused on the overall adequacy of finance systems and equity among school districts (Education Week, 2019). Tennessee became one of those states that had their funding formula challenged.

SCHOOL FINANCE IN TENNESSEE

The Tennessee Superintendent Study Council meets on an annual basis in Gatlinburg, Tennessee. A picturesque site that offers entertainment and fun for the family becomes the center of planning and professional development for superintendents.

Most of the superintendents in Tennessee attend the three-day conference that is hosted by the Tennessee Organization of School Superintendents (TOSS) and the Tennessee State Department of Education. The conference allows TOSS to have a formal meeting with their members, enables superintendents to interact with each other—the senior staff of the Tennessee Department of Education—to meet with the commissioner of education for a question and answer session, and for TOSS members to receive professional development that is specifically designed to enhance their job performance. The annual conference presents a unique opportunity of sharing and learning for the chief education officers of Tennessee.

During the 1986 Superintendent Study Council Conference, a small group of superintendents were having a discussion about the day's professional development sessions. The discussion quickly focused on the session where the Department of Education presented their budget for the 1986–1987 school year. As usual, the superintendents complained about the lack of money to educate students and to operate schools in their respective district.

One superintendent boldly made the suggestion that superintendents should sue the state of Tennessee for not adequately funding education. He further stated that he had researched this idea, and school districts in other states had sued their state governments based on inadequate funding. Poor school districts should get equitable and adequate funding to meet the mandates that are set by federal and state governments without causing a burden on the poor school districts.

After the discussion had ended, and the group of superintendents had disbanded, superintendents started receiving phone calls from two of the superintendents informing them of a meeting that would convene after the conference sessions had ended. The purpose of the meeting was to discuss school finance in Tennessee.

The historical meeting that occurred in 1986 was the genesis of the Tennessee Small Schools for Equity that later became the Tennessee School Systems for Equity (TSSE). Bill Emerson and Wayne Qualls became the leaders of the TSSE. Bill Emerson would become the chairman of the newly formed organization, and Wayne Qualls, who would later become the commissioner of education for Tennessee, is the current executive director of TSSE.

In 1988, a group of rural school districts, superintendents, board of education members, students, and parents filed suit claiming that Tennessee's education funding system violated Article XI, Section 12 of the Tennessee Constitution because the funding system denied public school students the right to an equal education that was due to a disparity in resources between rural and urban counties. Although TSSE had seventy-five members in the organization, only a representative group would be named in the lawsuit (Crockett, Grundy, Hancock, Hickman, Overton, Pickett, Trousdale, and Wayne Counties).

Small Schools I—The Tennessee Foundation Program

The first suit brought by the Tennessee Small Schools for Equity focused on the Tennessee Foundation Program (TFP). The TFP was the funding formula that Tennessee utilized to fund K–12 education in public schools.

In the initial lawsuit in 1988, the plaintiffs sought a declaratory judgment that the state's educational funding statutes were unconstitutional, that the defendants be enjoined from acting pursuant to those statutes, and that the state be required to formulate and establish a funding system that met the constitutional standards.

Not all school districts were in favor of suing the state of Tennessee; several school systems located in urban and suburban counties across the state (Davidson County, Chattanooga-Hamilton County, Knox County, Jackson-Madison County, Memphis City, Clarksville-Montgomery County, Sevier County, Shelby County, and Sullivan County) were allowed to intervene and oppose the plaintiff's suit on the premise that the funding scheme enacted by the legislature was not reviewable by the courts. In summary, the defendants argued that Article XI, Section 12, of the state constitution provided no qualitative standards for measuring the quality of education or the sufficiency of funding and that such matters were left to the exclusive province of the legislative and executive branches (Tennessee Small School Systems, et al. v. Ned Ray McWherter, et al., 1988).

The Supreme Court of Tennessee agreed with the trial court's findings that there were impermissible disparities in the educational opportunities available to public school students with evidence of significant differences in teacher qualifications, student performance, basic educational programs, and facilities. Many schools in rural districts had decaying physical science laboratories, outdated textbooks, and outdated libraries. Some of the school districts were unable to offer advanced placement courses, more than one foreign language, or the state-mandated art and music classes (Tennessee Small School Systems, et al. v. Ned Ray McWherter, et al., 1988)

The TFP was based primarily on average daily attendance of students, while local funding depended heavily on local sales tax collections, property tax, and discretionary funding by local governments. The Supreme Court of Tennessee had determined that the TFP included only a "token amount" of state funds for the equalization of school systems and rendered that the state funding formula (TFP) violated equal protection principles. Thus, the Tennessee Supreme Court opined, "The constitution imposes upon the General Assembly the obligation to maintain and support a system of free public schools that affords substantially equal education opportunities to all students" (Tennessee Small School Systems, al. v. Ned Ray McWherter, et al., 1988).

The TFP was broken, and the Tennessee legislature had the mandate from the court to establish a public school system that afforded a substantially equal educational opportunities to all students. An acceptable funding plan had to be created by the legislature that gave the management responsibilities to local governments, but not the funding burden.

The first legal challenge brought against the state of Tennessee was named by the court, Small Schools I. The premise of this case was based on equity and resulted in the creation and implementation of the Basic Education Program. Since the United States Constitution gave the obligation of establishing a free and public education to states, all states must address education in their constitutions. The Tennessee Constitution (1970) states that, "The state of Tennessee recognizes the inherent value of education and encourages its support. The General Assembly shall provide for the maintenance, support and eligibility standards of a system of free public schools. The General Assembly may establish and support such post-secondary educational institutions, including public institutions of higher learning, as it determines" (Tennessee Constitution, Article XI, Section12, 1972).

Small Schools II—The Basic Education Plan

In the Small School II, the plaintiffs contended that the state's new plan, which omitted teachers' salaries as a component of the Basic Education Program (BEP) and failed to equalize salaries, amounted to an unconstitutional denial of a substantially equal education opportunity to all students.

The BEP, which was enacted by the legislature while Small Schools II was pending in the Supreme Court, provided for allocation of funds to local school systems on a fair and equitable basis by recognizing the differences in the ability of local jurisdictions to raise local revenues (Tennessee Code Annotated 49-3-356). The BEP required both state and local funding, but with the proportionate local share determined by each county's relative ability to pay, or its fiscal capacity.

The BEP formula was based on the cost of forty-three components that the legislature deemed necessary for Tennessee schools to succeed (Tennessee Code Annotated, 49-3-302(3), Supplement,2001). The components included items such as the cost of vocational education, guidance counseling, textbooks, physical education, computer technology, transportation, library services, special education, art, music, classroom supplies, alternative schools, travel, and capital expenditures for facilities. The components also included the costs of hiring secretaries, nurses, librarians, social workers, principals and their assistants, assessment personnel, coordinators, supervisors, custodians, psychologists, and superintendents but, significantly, omitted the cost of hiring teachers, the most important component of any education plan and a major part of every education budget. In addition, the BEP formula included provisions for an annual review of the actual cost of each component and for reviewing the formula each year to make any adjustments for improving the system (Tennessee Small School Systems, et al. v. Ned Ray McWherter, et al., 1988).

The plaintiffs challenged the BEP formula based on the fact that costs associated with increasing or equalizing teachers' salaries was not one of the components that was deemed necessary for a school to succeed. The omission of the teacher salary component that was recommended by the Tennessee State Board of Education had caused a disparity in teachers' salaries across the state. The legislature had left that component out of the BEP.

The Supreme Court of Tennessee opined, "The omission of a requirement for equalizing teachers' salaries is a significant defect in the BEP and that the failure to provide for equalization of teachers' salaries according to the BEP formula, puts the entire plan at risk functionally and, therefore, legally." The Tennessee Small Schools for Equity had won this case, and the court ordered that the BEP had to include the equalization of teachers' salaries according to the BEP formula in order for the plan to be constitutional (Tennessee Small School Systems, et al. v. Ned Ray McWherter, et al., 1988).

Small Schools III—Salary Equity Plan

In 1995, the Tennessee legislature enacted the salary equity plan, which on a one-time basis attempted to equalize teachers' salaries in those school districts where the average salary was below $28,094 as of 1993 but did not include teachers' salaries as a component of the BEP. The BEP did not include provisions for annual review or cost determination of teachers' salaries. The plaintiffs filed action arguing that the legislature set an arbitrary floor for teachers' salaries and did not submit teachers' salaries to the annual review and cost determination process applicable to all of the other cost components under the BEP (Tennessee Small School Systems, et al. v. Ned Ray McWherter, et al., 1988).

After a two-day hearing, the trial court found that the state had met its constitutional obligation to equalize teachers' salaries and dismissed the action. TSSE did not accept the trial court's decision and appealed the decision to the Tennessee Supreme Court.

The Supreme Court of Tennessee held that the salary equity plan failed to satisfy the state's constitutional obligation to formulate and maintain a system of public education that affords substantially equal educational opportunity to all students. The trial court's judgment dismissing the case was reversed, and the case was remanded for such further proceedings as may be appropriate. Costs of the appeal were taxed to the defendants and intervenors for which execution may issue if necessary (Tennessee Small School Systems, et al. v. Ned Ray McWherter, et al., 1988).

The Tennessee Small School Systems have never lost a case or appeal that has been heard by the Supreme Court of Tennessee. The issue for Tennessee boards of education, parents, educators, and administrators has always been equity. However, the issue of adequacy of funding for public schools in Tennessee has never been addressed. Will adequacy of funding public education in Tennessee be the focus for TSSE in the future? Is TSSE finished with litigation, or are other legal challenges being constructed? One may only conclude that these questions will be answered sometime during the twenty-first century.

THE BASIC EDUCATION PROGRAM

The Basic Education Program (BEP) was adopted by the State Legislature in 1992 as part of the Education Improvement Act (EIA). As a result of the Tennessee Small Schools for Equity lawsuit, the BEP has replaced the old funding formula known as the Tennessee Foundation Program.

The BEP has two separate parts that operate in unison to determine the amount of revenue that each district is to receive:

1. The Tennessee Department of Education determines the amount of revenue based on the BEP formula for each school district.
2. The equalization or fiscal capacity that is based on the local's ability to pay is determined by the fiscal capacity indices that are provided by the Tennessee Advisor Commission on Intergovernmental Relations (TACIR) and the UT Center for Business and Economic Research (CBER)

GENERAL OVERVIEW OF BEP FORMULA

- The funds generated by the BEP are what the state has defined as sufficient to provide a basic level of education for Tennessee students. This basic level of funding includes both a state share of the BEP and a local share of the BEP.

- The BEP has four major categories (instruction, benefits, classroom, and non-classroom), each made up of separate components related to the basic needs of students, teachers, and administrators within a school system.
- Student enrollment (average daily membership) is the primary driver of funds generated by the BEP.
- There are forty-six BEP components, most of which are based on student enrollment (ADM). For example, students per teacher, assistant principals per school, or dollars per student for textbooks.
- Unit cost adjustments (salary, health benefits, insurance) are essential to maintaining a similar level of funding from year to year, due to inflation. For example, in 2006 over 100 million new state dollars were required to maintain full funding of the BEP.
- The funds generated by the BEP are divided into state and local shares for each of the four major categories (instructional, instructional benefits, classroom).
- The state and local share for each school system is based on an equalization formula that is applied to the BEP. This equalization formula is the primary factor in determining how much of the BEP is supported by the state vs. the local district.
- The equalization formula is driven primarily by property values and sales tax, applied at a county level. For example, the state and local equalization shares for County System A would be the exact same

state and local shares for City System A, within the same county.

- All local school systems are free to raise additional education dollars beyond the funds generated by the BEP.
- Average Daily Membership (ADM) drives the formula and is funded on prior year's ADM.
- ADM generates positions teachers, supervisors, teaching assistants, school secretaries, custodians, and principals.
- ADMs are multiplied by the unit cost for supplies, equipment, textbooks, travel, capital outlay, etc. The unit cost is determined by a using a three-year average and inflated up two years. The unit cost for textbooks is a three-year average that is inflated up one year. Unit cost for alternative schools, duty free lunch, and maintenance and operations use the prior year value and inflated up one year.
- Capital outlay cost for the school district is determined by the square footage cost obtained from the *RS Means* publication. The cost is determined when each ADM generates square footage, multiplied by the cost, then amortized to arrive at a yearly cost. Capital outlay includes architect fees and equipment.
- The fiscal capacity of a school district (local ability to pay) is determined by the TACIR and the UT CBER models.

- The TACIR model utilizes four factors in a complex multiple-regression model.
    1. Property tax base
    2. Sales tax case
    3. Per capita personal income
    4. Equalized residential and farm assessment
- The UT CBER model is based on property and sales tax bases. This model is utilized in the BEP 2.0.
- Currently, a TACIR and CBER mix is used in the BEP calculation. Fifty percent is TACIR, and 50 percent is CBER. Tennessee is moving toward using the CBER model and omitting the TACIR model. When the state uses the CBER model for 100 percent of the calculation of a county's fiscal capacity, a majority of the rural school districts will lose revenue from the state. The urban school districts gain revenue from the state of Tennessee.
- Funding months for the BEP are August (12.5 percent), October (17.5 percent), April (35 percent), and June (35 percent).

MAINTENANCE OF EFFORT

The maintenance of effort requirement prevents a local government from reducing its share of local funding for schools as a direct result of increased state funding. No local education agency shall submit a budget to local legislative body that directly supplants or proposes to use state funds to supplant any local current operation funds, excluding capital outlay and debt service (Tennessee Code Annotated 49.2-203(a)(11)(A)(ii); 49—314(c)(3)(A)).

At the beginning of a new budget year, the Tennessee State Department of Education uses a supplanting test to insure the maintenance of local effort for each school district. Budgeted local revenue must be equal to or greater than the previous year's budgeted amount, unless ADMs have decreased.

FUND BALANCE

Each school district must maintain a 3 percent fund balance that is not dedicated to a particular category or line-item in the school district's budget. If budget expenditures exceed revenues, a local education agency must have 3 percent of operating expenditures in the fund balance before the budget will be approved by the Tennessee State Department of Education.

The use of a fund balance is governed by statute. After the adoption of the operating budget funds, ".... Funds shall be available to offset shortfalls of budgeted revenues....and .... to meet unforeseen increases in operating expenses" (TCA 49-3-352(c)). Funds beyond the accumulated fund balance that are in excess of 3 percent of the budgeted annual operating expenses for the current fiscal year may be budgeted and expended for any education purposes. These funds must be recommended by the board of education prior to appropriation by local legislative body.

There is not a requirement to have a 3 percent of operating expenditures in the fund balance. However, the Local Education Agency cannot use the fund balance unless the fund balance exceeds 3 percent of operating expenditures.

STABILITY PROVISION

The stability provision is implemented when the total state BEP funds that a Tennessee school district generates in the current school year are less than the total state BEP funds generated the previous school year. This situation usually results from a decline in student enrollment (ADMs). The Tennessee State Department of Education then provides a one-year grace period before funding is reduced.

MANDATORY INCREASE

This BEP provision allows school districts on stability to receive additional funds for state-mandated increases in salary, Tennessee Consolidated Retirement System contributions, and health insurance. The Local Education Agency also receives the mandatory increase amount for each BEP-generated position.

The BEP handbook is provided for the reader. Annually, the handbook is updated by the Tennessee Department of Education and approved by the Tennessee State Board of Education. Each school district downloads the handbook for school board members, superintendents, budget directors, and assistant superintendents of finance. The BEP handbook becomes one of the key sources for building the Local Education Agency's budget.

This handbook lists the BEP components and the cost specifications for each component. The components include both operating and capital outlay costs.

The BEP components serve as the basis for calculating the level of funding for each school system. While the components provide the basis for calculating the level of BEP funding for each local school district, the BEP does not prescribe specific levels of expenditures for individual components. Total costs are calculated by applying cost specifications to the districts' average daily memberships.

Equalization shares responsibility among the local school systems and the state based on variations in the cost of delivering services to students and in relative fiscal capacity.

THE BASIC EDUCATION HANDBOOK

EDUCATIONAL SALARY COMPONENTS (STATE)

COMPONENT FUNDING LEVEL

REGULAR EDUCATION TEACHER

1 per 20 ADM K-3
1 per 25 ADM 4-6
1 per 25 ADM 7-9
1 per 22.08 ADM 10-12

Career & Technical Education Teacher	1 per 16.67 career technical education FTEADM
Special Education Teacher	(Caseload Allocations)

(number of students identified and served = I & S)

Option 1	91.0
Option 2 and 3	58.5
Option 4, 5, and 6	16.5
Option 7, 8, 9, and 10	8.5

Elementary Counselor	1 per 500 ADM K – 6 **
Secondary Counselor	1 per 350 ADM 7 – 12 (Including CTE) **

Elementary Art Teacher	1 per 525 ADM K – 6
Elementary Music Teacher	1 per 525 ADM K – 6
Elementary Physical Education Teacher	1 per 350 ADM K – 4 1 per 265 ADM 5 – 6
Elementary Librarian (K – 8)	.5 per school < 265 1 per school 265 – 439 1 per school 440 – 659 (+.5 assistant) 1 per school > 660 (+1 assistant)
Secondary Librarian (9 – 12)	.5 per school < 300 1 per school 300 – 999 2 per school 1,000 – 1,499 2 per school > 1500 (+1 per add'l 750)
ELL Instructor	1 per 20 EL Students I & S
ELL Translator	1 per 200 EL Students I & S

INSTRUCTIONAL SALARY COMPONENTS
(STATE SHARE = 70 percent)

COMPONENT FUNDING LEVEL

PRINCIPAL
.5 per school < 225 ***
1 per school > 225

ASSISTANT PRINCIPAL ELEMENTARY
.5 per school 660 – 879
1 per school 880 – 1,099
1.5 per school 1,100 – 1,319
2 per school > 1,320

ASSISTANT PRINCIPAL SECONDARY
.5 per school 300 – 649
1 per school 650 – 999
1.5 per school 1,000 – 1,249
2 per school > 1,250 (+1 per add'l 250)

SYSTEMWIDE INSTRUCTIONAL SUPERVISOR
1 per < 500 total ADM
2 per 500 – 999 total ADM
3 per 1,000 – 1,999 total ADM
3 per > 2,000 ADM (+1 per add'l 1,000)

CAREER & TECHNICAL EDUCATION SUPERVISOR	1 per 1,000 Career & Technical education FTEADM
SPECIAL EDUCATION SUPERVISOR	1 per 750 special education I & S
SPECIAL EDUCATION ASSESSMENT PERSONNEL	1 per 600 special education I & S
SOCIAL WORKER	1 per 2,000 total ADM **
PSYCHOLOGIST	1 per 2,500 total ADM **
RESPONSE TO INSTRUCTION AND INTERVENTION (RTI)	1 per 2,750 total ADM (minimum 1 per system)

INSTRUCTIONAL BENEFITS COMPONENTS (STATE SHARE = 70 percent)

STAFF BENEFITS *	7.65 percent of BEP salary for FICA and Medicare
COMPONENT FUNDING LEVEL	
STAFF INSURANCE *	$7,236.26 per BEP position for insurance

Staff Retirement *	10/30 percent of BEP salary per licensed position OR 7.54 percent of BEP salary per classified position for TCRS

CLASSROOM COMPONENTS
(STATE SHARE = 75 percent)

COMPONENT FUNDING LEVEL

K – 12 AT-RISK	$915.25 per identified at-risk ADM. Funded at 100 percent at-risk.
TEXTBOOKS	$77.50 per total ADM

CLASSROOM MATERIALS & SUPPLIES
(incudes fee waiver)

$86.75 per regular ADM
$157.75 per career & technical education FTEADM
$36.50 per special education I & S
$51.77 per Academic exit exam (12th grade)
$18.45 per Technical exit exam (1/4 CTE)

Instructional Equipment	$69.50 per regular ADM
	$99.75 per CTE FTEADM
	$17.25 per special education I & S
Classroom-Related Travel	$16.00 per regular ADM
	$50.50 per CTE FTEADM
	$17.25 per special education I & S
CTE Center for Transportation	For participating systems to transport students to career and technical center attended part of the day.
Technology	$41.30 per funded ADM
Nurses	1 per 3,000 total ADM (minimum 1 per system)
Instructional Assistant	1 per 75 ADM K – 6

Special Education Assistant	1 per 60 special education students I & S Options 5, 7, 8
Substitute Teacher	$64.25 per total ADM
Alternative School	$3.75 per total ADM K – 12 plus $34.25 per ADM 7 – 12 (including CTE)

NON-CLASSROOM COMPONENTS
(STATE SHARE = 50 percent)

COMPONENT FUNDING LEVEL

SUPERINTENDENT 1 per county ****

SYSTEM SECRETARIAL SUPPORT
1 per system < 500
2 per system 500 – 1,250
3 per system 1,251 – 1,999
3 per system 1,999 and above, plus 1 for each add'l 1,000 ADM

School Secretaries	.5 per school < 225 1 per school 225 – 374 1 per school > 375 (plus 1 per each add'l 375)

Technology Coordinators	1 per system with one add'l for each 6,400 ADM
Maintenance & Operations	100 sq. ft. per total K – 4 ADM 110 sq. ft. per total 5 – 8 ADM 130 sq. ft. per total 9 – 12 ADM Total sq. ft. X $3.55/sq. ft. **** 1 Custodian per 22,376 calculated sq. ft.
Non-Instructional Equipment	$26.50 per total ADM
Pupil Transportation	Allocated to systems that provide transportation. Formula is established by Commissioner of Education and based on number of pupils transported, miles transported, and density of pupils per route mile.

Staff Benefits and Insurance	$6,753.85 per BEP position for insurance OR $10,130.77 for superintendent and technology coordinator; plus 7.65 percent of BEP salary for FICA and Medicare. Add 10.30 percent of BEP salary per superintendent and technology coordinator OR 7.545 of BEP salary per classified position for TCRS.
Capital Outlay	100 sq. ft. per total K – 4 ADM x $139.41 / sq. ft. 110 sq. ft. per total 5 – 8 ADM x $140.00 / sq. ft. 130 sq. ft. per total 9 – 12 ADM x $149.73 / sq. ft. Add equipment (10 percent of sq. ft. cost) Add architect's (7 percent of sq. ft. cost)

Capital Outlay	Add debt service (20 yrs. @ 6.00 percent)
	Divide total by 40 yrs. = annual amount

SALARIES USED IN BEP CALCULATIONS

TEACHERS AND OTHER LICENSED PERSONNEL

The BEP allocation for salaries for each school system is based on:

The number of each type of position generated by the cost components the current salary unit cost for instructional personnel = $48,330 average annual superintendent salary = $115,700 per county

OTHER PERSONNEL

Average annual library/instructional assistant salary = $24,100 average annual custodian salary = $25,900
Average annual school secretary salary = $33,800
Average annual system secretary salary = $43,200

FOOTNOTES

** If a system within a county having more than one system does not have enough pupils to qualify for a position, the relevant county totals are used, and each system receives a pro rata share based on its proportion of total relevant enrollment. If county totals are not sufficient to generate a position, the county is allocated one position and each system is allocated a pro rata share of the position based on its proportion of the relevant enrollment.

***Elementary schools < 100 are not allocated a principal.

****One superintendent is allocated for each county. If there is more than one school system in a county, each system receives a pro rata share based on its proportion of total county ADM.

*****For purposes of calculating benefits and insurance: for maintenance add 60 percent of sq. ft. cost to salary allocation; for pupil transportation add 45 percent of amount to salary allocation. Apply calculated rate (insurance, FICA, TCRS) for classified personnel as specified to 60 percent or 45 percent of allocation, respectively.

CONCLUSION

The BEP would have never become a reality without Bill Emerson and Wayne Qualls. Both of these retired superintendents were founders of the TSSE. Without their leadership, the state of Tennessee would never have been challenged in the court system, and our school districts would have never achieved a pathway of equity for educating the students of Tennessee.

Has Tennessee solved the problem with funding equity in Tennessee, and is future litigation feasible to pursue for school districts? The answer is yes to both of these questions. Funding is always going to be an obstacle for school districts in Tennessee, but the existence of the TSSE that has more than 80 Tennessee school districts as members will always monitor school funding on a constant continuum.

The BEP should always be monitored and updated to meet the changes in the education environment and teaching the students of Tennessee. It is highly probable that the Tennessee BEP will be updated to meet equity and adequacy in the future. To accomplish this purpose in the past, the directors of school have utilized litigation to purse and achieve equity in schools. One must assume that this course of action will be utilized in the future to achieve, not only equity, but adequacy of education funding.

CLASS ACTIVITIES

- Read and answer the questions at end of the case study.

HOW MANY TEACHERS DO I NEED FOR MY SCHOOL?

Thomas Reacher was appointed the assistant principal at Jerad Elementary School. Thomas obtained his specialist of education degree from Administrator Memorial University in 2017 and has been an assistant principal for three years.

As assistant principal, Mr. Reacher implemented and supervised student discipline for the largest elementary school in the Oz County School District. Other duties that were assigned to Thomas were principal designee for Individualized Educational Plan Team Meetings and cafeteria monitor. Since he did an outstanding job in the performance of these duties, the Oz County Board of Education appointed him the principal of the newly constructed Consolidated Elementary School.

The Consolidated Elementary School had 875 students enrolled in a school that was built to house 1,000 (K–6) students. Every student had a computer, and every teacher had a computer workstation in their classroom. In accordance with the district's strategic plan, the school district had consolidated four smaller schools with the same grade configuration into the new elementary school.

Thomas Reacher was happy with his promotion that came with a $10,000 salary improvement. Life was good until the director of schools requested that Jack calculate the number of teachers and assistant principals needed for the new school.

The beginning enrollment for the current school year is 875 students. The enrollment for each grade at Consolidated Elementary is:

- 1st Grade–135 students
- 2nd Grade–180 students
- 3rd Grade–163 students
- 4th Grade–124 students
- 5th Grade–146 students
- 6th Grade–127 students

Questions:

1. How many classroom teachers did the principal need for each grade level?

2. How many assistant principals did the principal need for his school?

3. What is the total number of personnel that the principal needs to staff his school?

- Why did Tennessee superintendents resort to litigation in achieving equity in Tennessee's public schools?

- Should there be "winners" and "losers" in funding Tennessee schools? Explain your answer.

- Why did Tennessee superintendents file a lawsuit against the state of Tennessee on three different occasions? Explain each lawsuit.

- Interview a Tennessee director of schools on the topic of funding education in Tennessee Schools.

- Analyze the BEP to determine the program's strengths and weaknesses.

- Interview a Tennessee principle on the topic of funding education in her/his school.

- BEP Exercise: Divide the class into Professional Learning Committees. Each group is to determine the number of licensed and non-licensed people that would be needed to operate a school of 896 students with a grade configuration of K–8. Each PLC must utilize the BEP guidelines and the Tennessee Department of Education Rules & Regulations as a resource.

CHAPTER 6

THE SCHOOL DISTRICT BUDGET

According to George E. Ridler and Robert J. Shockley (1989), "A rich background in administration, curriculum, and instruction is essential for a superintendent of schools to be successful" (Shockley, 1989, p. 3). However, no other phase of the job tests his or her leadership ability than the annual budget.

The director of schools is the chief education officer (CEO) of a school district. She or he is responsible for the preparing and presenting the school district's budget to the board of education and funding body (county commission or city council) for the school district. The Tennessee superintendent executes this responsibility on an annual basis.

In constructing a school district budget, it is important to do the following:

1. Review the state rules and regulations that govern the operation of schools in a school district.

2. Review the Basic Education Program (BEP).
3. Implement a needs analysis for the school district.
4. Schedule meetings to obtain input from the school personnel, teacher associations, retired teacher association, community leaders, elected officials, businesses, and industry leaders.
5. Utilize the adopted format by the school board and Tennessee to display the budget.
6. Communicate the budget to the board, local funding body, school personnel, and community in an understandable and transparent rhetoric.

REVIEW OF TENNESSEE'S RULES AND REGULATIONS FOR EDUCATION

The importance of reviewing and becoming knowledgeable of Tennessee's framework for the operation and governance of schools cannot not be overstated. If the superintendent has never been an administrator in Tennessee, the review of this resource becomes more significant. Without this knowledge the director of schools will not and should not attempt to construct a budget for presentation to the school board.

REVIEW THE BASIC EDUCATION PROGRAM

If the director of schools does not know the number of personnel that she/he will be funded from the state of Tennessee, the school district assumes the risk of hiring personnel that the district must pay from their local funds. For example, each teacher that is hired outside of the BEP guidelines will not receive funding from the state for that teacher. If the district does not receive state funding for these teachers, the cost will be astronomical for the school district (100 teachers X $30, 000 average salary for first year teacher = $3,000,000 of local funding).

State funding for school districts is based on the county's wealth. School districts that are poor may receive 90 percent of their funding from the state. Wealthy school districts will receive less state funding that may be as low as 45 percent. A director of schools must know the fiscal capacity (determined by the TACIR and CBER calculation models) of their school district to determine the amount of revenue for their school district.

NEEDS ANALYSIS FOR SCHOOL DISTRICT

The director of schools must create a budget that has feedback from all constituents within the school district. If adequate feedback is given from citizens in the county or city that the school district resides, the superintendent's passage of the school district budget becomes easier. The school budget becomes the people's budget because everyone has ownership in the assembling of the school budget.

Today, the soliciting and receiving feedback from the public is not difficult. The twenty-first century is an informational society. Every parent, student, and home has a mobile phone, TV, computer, and radio. It is easy to communicate with people. Messages soliciting feedback on educational issues and receiving responses is a simple task to perform in today's society.

To find the educational priorities that are prevalent in the county or city that the school district serves, the director of schools must do the following:

1. Using a sampling of the residents of your school district, send a detailed questionnaire to be completed by these individuals and analyze the results. The analysis may be done by a consulting firm or the school staff.
2. Local school forums may be utilized to gather data. As director of schools, schedule a forum that specifically addresses next year's budget. The school board, city council, and county commission should be invited. The message should be very clear and specific about the topic of the meeting.
3. The internet is utilized to send a brief survey to parents of each school in the district. The survey should only address the school budget.
4. A plethora of meetings should be scheduled by the director of schools that are focused on next year's school budget. The meetings should be scheduled with the finance committees of the county, city, and school board. The director should also include the Parents and Teachers Organization or Parents and Teachers Association officers of each school, the athletic booster clubs at each school, the teacher

union leaders, the retired teacher association, business and industry leaders (Chamber of Commerce), and the senior citizens association.

5. Create a speaker's bureau to speak to the service clubs (Rotary, Kiwanis, Lions). Service clubs are always needing monthly speakers. Volunteer to supply a monthly speaker to the service clubs to talk about educational topics (budget, curriculum and instruction, accountability).
6. Utilize the media to address educational topics (budget, school discipline, social media in the school environment).
7. Conduct workshops with the board of education, finance committee of the county commission or city council, and elected officials of the county.
8. The director should know the desires of the school board. Have frank discussions with individual board members and seek approval from the board to have an annual retreat away from the school district with the new budget as an item on the agenda. Remember that the retreat is a workshop setting and not a board meeting that requires a vote for any action on any items on the agenda. Follow school board policy on workshops; the school board secretary may or may not need to advertise the meeting.

Following this process, the director of schools should have the necessary feedback needed to create a school budget and now has a framework to begin working in concert with the board to develop a school budget.

If the director of schools has goals that she/he have formulated, those goals need to be presented to the board before the creation of the budget. School boards dislike surprises. Making the school board aware of your goals will give your financial plan a much warmer reception.

BUDGET DESIGN

There are a variety of budget designs that exist for displaying the budget. Buzz words and an alphabet stew of letters (e.g., program, line item, ZZB, PPBS) abound in budgeting, just as in other areas. The main focus of the school board's budget is not the system used but rather the projection of a professionally planned and articulated budget that will serve the needs of the school system, governmental officials, and the public.

Tennessee utilizes a combination of budget designs. The Program Budget System and the Line-Item Budget designs are used for state government, county governments, local governments, and schools. Both designs yield advantages because both designs simplify the work of the budget office by displaying and presenting budget data.

The Program Budget System is designed to identify the cost of programs. It often incorporates a line-item budget as a subset of each program. This budget design makes it possible for the Board of Education and the public to make comparisons and judgements for the appropriateness for concerning the appropriateness of expenditures for the system's programs. For example, is the school district spending too much revenue on competitive sports and not enough on reading or improvement of test scores?

The Line-Item Budget is designed to simplify accounting procedures, budget monitoring, and reporting procedures for the staff, the board of education, and the public. This budget design consolidates each category into a "line."

By using both budget designs and adding accurate expenditures that were expended the previous two years by category (program) and expenditure (line-item), the school board and directors of school have an excellent display for preparation, presentation, and monitoring the school budget. The display of category and expenditure for each line-item within the category is understandable and reasonably transparent when actual expenditures for the previous two years are on the budget document.

The budget should be easy to understand and to display what the board and director have done in the past, and what the school district plans to do next year. The director and board should be prepared to explain why line items are reduced, eliminated, added, or increased. Any modification made to next year's budget needs to have a detailed explanation with data to verify the rationale for the modifications.

A Tennessee school district's budget has the following elements:

- Estimated Revenues and Other Sources Summary

- Estimated Revenues and Other Sources Detail
- Estimated State Revenues
- Estimated Federal Revenues
- Reserves and Fund Balances
- Estimated Expenditures and Total Expenditures for Each Category/Program
- Previous Year Budget Actuals
- Previous Year Approved Budget
- Proposed School Year Budget
- Comparison of Previous Year Budget to Proposed Budget
- Budget Notes

A TENNESSEE SCHOOL DISTRICT BUDGET

An example of a Tennessee school budget is displayed on the websites of Tennessee school districts. It is recommended that the reader/student observes the district's budget to enhance their familiarity of a typical Tennessee budget document.

BUDGET CALENDAR

The budget calendar should begin in February of the current budget year for the construction of next year's budget. Since the budget year for Tennessee school districts must be submitted to the funding body (county commission or city council) by July 1 for approval, the February date should give ample time for budget request forms from staff personnel and public input.

The following calendar is suggested to serve as an example for a Tennessee director of schools and school board to follow. Dates are arbitrary, but the months are highly recommended.

SAMPLE BUDGET CALENDAR

- February 15—Budget preparation begins by reviewing the current budget with the district's budget director.
- March 1—Budget request forms are sent to principals, supervisors, directors, assistant superintendents, and associate superintendents.
- April 15–17—Board retreat is planned for a budget workshop.
- May 12—Due date for student enrollment projection and staffing requests from all schools.
- May 17—Due date for budget requests from schools and central office personnel.
- May 18—Inventory reports are due from schools and central office personnel.
- May 19—Schedule budget meetings with public to solicit input.
- May 27—Review data that has been collected from the public, businesses, and civic organizations.

- June 1—Completed student enrollment projection for school district is due from school attendance supervisor.
- June 2—Review budget requests with supervisors.
- June 3—Review budget requests with principals.
- June 8—Board workshop is held to discuss next year's school budget.
- June 9—A joint meeting with the funding body finance committee (county commission or city council) and school board to discuss the school budget.
- June 10—Director of schools presents budget to the school board in an announced school board meeting.
- June 12—A joint meeting with the finance committee (county commission or city council) and school board to discuss the school budget.
- June 15—Budget hearing is held by the board for public review and comments.
- June 18—School board adopts next year's school budget.
- June 20—The adopted budget is presented to the funding body (county commission or city council) for adoption.
- July 1—County or city adopts budget for entire county or city operation that includes the school district's budget.

Since most Tennessee school districts request more funds each budget year, it is not an unusual circumstance for a funding body to delay the approval of the school budget. The delay of funding the school budget comes as a result of the funding body's attempt to minimize the tax burden on the local taxpayers. An approval delay in the school district's budget has the potential of having catastrophic consequences. Tennessee school districts must have an approved school budget to the Tennessee Department of Education Department by October 1. If this mandate is not met, the state stops disbursing state funds on a monthly basis to school districts, most school districts would not be able to continue the teaching and learning environment without these monthly state funds.

CONCLUSION

It is the responsibility of the director of schools to construct a budget calendar, determine the needs of the school district, solicit input from all stakeholders, and construct a budget. The process that the superintendent implements to achieve this responsibility is crucial for receiving approval from the school board and the funding body (county commission or city council).

The director of schools should review the financial report (end-of-year report of what was budgeted and expended by the school district), the budget documents of the previous and current school year, and the five-year strategic plan for the school district. Follow the budget calendar and work with the assistant director of finance and the chair or president of the school board.

The director should be prepared to present the new budget to the public, the school board, and to the funding body. At this stage of preparation, the director of schools should know what the needs of the school are and what the public is willing to support. If the school district does not need a tax increase for the new budget, the director should have a school budget that is easily approved by the funding body. However, if a tax increase is needed to achieve the school district's goals, I recommend the following:

1. Prepare talking points based on the needs in the budget.
2. Prepare a slide presentation for the stakeholders to build support for the district's budget.
3. Talk with each member of the board of education and funding body members. Listen to their comments and determine what they support and do not support. Do this task before the formal presentation to the board and funding body.
4. In agreement with the board of education, be prepared to negotiate and prioritize the school district's needs. Is a salary improvement for teachers more important than expansion of the seating at the high school football stadium? Are the school board and director of schools amenable to reducing the

requested tax increase by reducing the teachers' salary improvement from 3 percent to 2 percent?

CLASS ACTIVITIES

- Read the case and answer the following questions.
    1. What are the ramifications for the school district in the reduction of the tax appropriation for schools? Explain your answer.
    2. What actions should the school board and director of schools employ in response to the county commission's reduction of the school tax increase? Explain your answer.

CASE STUDY

In July 1980, a superintendent was appointed to his first position as chief education officer for a rural school district. He was to assume his new position on September 1, 1980. The new superintendent had approximately thirty days to leave his principal's position and to assume the role as a director of schools in Tennessee.

The new director of schools first ten days on the job would be crucial to his success or failure in the new position. Although he had a three-year contract, the incoming superintendent knew that getting to know his inherited administrative team that consisted of supervisors and principals would be a challenge. He felt that he was up to the task. He would evaluate his administrative cabinet and, if needed, make changes at the end of the school year.

His checklist for preparing for the new job was to read the board policies, review the strategic plan for the school district, review the Tennessee State Board of Education Rules and Regulations Manual, and to review the existing and new Tennessee statutes that governed education. Plus, the new director of schools was going to schedule an open forum at each school in the evening to enable parents and staff to meet him.

The budget was approved, and the school year had begun. The new budget gave the teachers a 5 percent local salary improvement, teachers and support staff have been hired, and school equipment and supplies have been purchased. The new superintendent simply had to supervise personnel and manage the school budget.

In January of 1981, the county commission met and reduced the school budget and lowered the tax rate by 50 cents. Forty cents of the tax rate had been appropriated to the school district and included the salary improvement for teachers.

- Utilizing the current school budget document for your school district, prepare a slide presentation to present to the school board and the county commission.
- As director of schools, compose a sample letter of instructions and budget request form that you would submit to your assistant directors, supervisors, and principals.

CHAPTER 7

THE SCHOOL BUDGET

Budgeting at the school level is not an exhaustive process for Tennessee principals. The format of the budget and the accounting principles were adopted for schools in 1959 by the Tennessee legislature, and the Tennessee Internal School Uniform Accounting Policy Manual (TAPM) is now required reading for principals.

The School Accounting Act enables local school boards to authorize an individual school to receive money for student activities and other events and establishes a student activity and other internal school funds as the property of the respective schools. The act also provides local boards of education and principals with definite authority and responsibility for the proper administration and safekeeping of all such internal school funds (Tennessee Department of Education Office of Local Finance, Section 1 – Page 1, 2011).

The TAPM encompasses both accounting procedures and administrative polices to bring local school boards into compliance with Section 49-2110, TCA. All school boards of public education must adopt this manual and codify the manual in their board policies. All principals of public schools are responsible for utilizing the manual in conducting the financial operations of their schools.

If the bookkeeper is found guilty of fraud, the principal is responsible. The principal must prove that he/she followed the procedures and guidelines that the manual required by statute and board policy. The principal must demonstrate that internal was evident and that expenditures are congruent with the school budget. If the principal has not managed the accounting and dispensing of school revenues in accordance with the TAPM, the school district has the authority to demote or terminate the principal.

All Tennessee school districts have board policy manuals that will contain a section pertaining to fiscal management. The Fiscal Management section of the school board manual will address all areas that pertain to the budget and includes the TAPM.

It is the responsibility of the school's principal to read and follow this manual. After thoroughly reading the TAPM, the principal, especially a new principal, needs to meet with the bookkeeper of the school and review the audit report of the previous school year and this year's school budget. This meeting should assist the principal in determining any audit findings that need to be monitored and to familiarize himself/herself with this year's budget.

Boards of education should develop board policies that govern fiscal management in school districts. The following principles must be adhered to when developing fiscal policy for internal school funds:

1. Money raised by students must be used to finance normal and legitimate extracurricular activities. Student activity funds should be used to supplement and not replace funds necessary to fulfill the local board's obligation to provide an instructional program, property, equipment, and salaries.
2. Money or property received by a school official, employee or volunteer, acting in his or her official capacity, becomes public school money or property. The money is the property of the respective school. Such money must be appropriately managed and safeguarded by the school.
3. Activities or events that generate student activity money should, in general, contribute to educational experience of students and should not conflict with, but add to, the school's instructional program.
4. School fundraising and the use of school facilities or equipment for the raising of internal school money should be in accordance with the school system's policies. The cost of using school facilities should be considered in drafting these policies. In the absence of related board of education policies, school fundraising is prohibited.
5. Money restricted for the use of a specific group should be spent in such a way as to benefit those

students currently in school who have contributed to the accumulation of such money.

6. Whenever possible, student body representation should be required in order to enhance the democratic management of student activity money to be raised and expended by, or for, the student body.
7. Activities and events organized to raise funds for either the student body as a whole or for a select or special group or segment of the student body shall be conducted on a voluntary basis only. Students who do not participate in such activities or events shall not be punished or discriminated against in any way. Likewise, a student's grade shall not be affected as a direct result of participation and, or lack of participation in, any fund-raising activities or events (Finance, 2011, Section 1-5, 1-6).

The TAPM defines the responsibilities of individual school principal. The school principal's responsibilities include, but are not limited to the following:

1. Notifying the Comptroller of the Treasury, Division of Municipal Audit, at (615) 741-1871, if the principal becomes aware of any evidence of fraud related to internal school funds;
2. Implementing and complying with the regulations, standards, and procedures contained in the manual and any other policies adopted by the local board of education that has jurisdiction over the school;

3. Providing for the safekeeping and handling of all school money and other school property, irrespective of the source of such money or property (Section 49-2-110, TCA);
4. Submitting reports and other materials to the director of schools or board of education on a timely basis, as directed;
5. Delivering all financial records, books, ledgers, computer files, reports, and supporting documentation, as directed by the director of schools or board of education;
6. Assuming responsibility for equipment located at the school, including equipment security, inventory control, care, and utilization;
7. Complying with purchasing procedures prescribed by the board of education, including bid policies and procedures established by the board for student activity and other internal school funds;
8. Notifying the director of schools or the director's designee and appropriate local law enforcement agency when equipment is stolen, misplaced, or destroyed;
9. Complying with the provisions of Section 49-6-2007, Tennessee Code Annotated, regarding the disposition or transfer of property; and

10. Maintain a current edition of the manual on school premises and make the manual available to all school personnel (Finance, 2011, Section 3-4).

The director of schools, school board, school bookkeeper, and the school principal have responsibilities. These responsibilities must not and cannot be ignored. If these responsibilities are ignored, the annual audit report will exhibit findings that will be reported to state officials for corrective action.

Generally, each school has only three fund types: (1) general fund, (2) restricted fund, and (3) food service fund. Therefore, the principal of the school should be familiar with these terms and utilize the TAPM that contains the proper forms for the school budget, chart of accounts, receiving revenue from funding sources, and disbursing revenue from the school's budget.

GENERAL FUND

The general fund is used to account for all money to be used for the general operation of the school or for the welfare of the student body. This includes, but is not limited to, allocations, locker fees, parking fees, library fines, rental income, unallocated interest income, school-wide fundraisers, and donations without stipulations.

All expenditures from the general fund must benefit the school or must contribute to the welfare of the student body and supplement and not replace funds necessary to fulfill the local board's obligation to provide an instructional program, property, equipment, and salaries. Expenditures meeting these criteria are restricted in purpose only as directed by the board of education, general laws and regulations, and school policies.

The general fund consists of separate revenue accounts and expenditure accounts. Total general fund expenditures (including unpaid obligations as of June 30 each year) must not exceed the beginning fund balance plus current year revenue. A deficit balance in the general fund (representing the net total of all account balances in the general fund) is not allowable. The principal is considered to be the sponsor of the general fund (Finance, 2011).

RESTRICTED FUND

The restricted fund is used to account for all money that is restricted for the use of a specific group (club, class, etc.) or legally restricted for a specific purpose (BEP funds, scholarship donations, etc.). The restricted fund may also be used for grants, donations, and awards in which the intended purpose does not fall under the scope of the General Fund (Governor's Award, performance incentive money, certain corporate donations, etc.). All expenditures of the restricted fund account money must be for the purpose or group for which the money was raised.

The restricted fund consists of accounts that include both revenues and expenditures, and each account maintains its own identity. Expenditures in each restricted fund account must not exceed the beginning balance plus current year revenue. A deficit balance in a restricted fund account is not allowable (Finance, 2011).

The principal may be the sponsor of some restricted fund accounts, such as legally restricted scholarships, grants, and donations. The principal generally designates other individuals as sponsors of club, class, and other restricted fund accounts (Finance, 2011).

FOOD SERVICE FUND

Each school that receives state and/or federal food service money for the purpose of financing food service operations must establish a separate fund entitled "Food Service Fund." This fund must be used to account for such money in accordance with state and federal rules and regulations governing food service programs. In most instances, the cafeteria manager is considered the sponsor of the food service fund (Finance, 2011).

ACCOUNTING FOR ATHLETICS

Although athletic programs may benefit the welfare of the student body, money raised from sanctioned athletic programs is generally restricted for the use of the athletic program. In addition, parents and other individuals generally demand a separate accounting of money raised by school athletics. Therefore, a sanctioned athletic program must be accounted for in the restricted fund. The board of education must determine which of the following alternatives for athletic accounting will be used by each school (Finance, 2011).

CHART OF ACCOUNTS

The chart of accounts provides uniform account numbers for individual schools to simplify the process of accounting, budgeting, and reporting by providing a consistent and uniform categories and objects cross the state for public schools.

The chart of accounts is divided into five categories:

1. Assets
2. Liabilities
3. Fund Balance
4. Revenues
5. Expenditures

These five categories will be present in the TAPM and located on the school budget form inside the manual.

Revenue accounts have at least four digits (302.1). The source of the revenue is indicated by the first three digits. For example, 302 gives the source of revenue as gate receipts. The last digit (1) is revenue that was derived from students viewing the movie. Thus, the code, 302.1, proves to the auditor that the revenue was obtained from gate receipts from the showing of a movie.

Expenditure accounts have at least 5 digits (406.12). The first 3 digits, 406, indicate the category, while the last two digits, 12, indicate the expenditure object code (Huss, 2009). For example, 406 shows the category is entertainment, and the last two digits, 12, reveal the expenditure object code was used for supplies and materials. The middle school had a play and paid for supplies and materials for the production of the play.

Sources of revenue and examples of acceptable expenditures are found in the TAPM. The TAPM may be viewed and downloaded for free at the following internet address: https://comptoller.tn.gov/content/dam/cot/la/documents/InternalSchoolUniformPolicy.pdf

CONCLUSION

The similarity between the school budget and the district budget are easily distinguishable and should not be confused. The district budget is broader in scope and is utilized for the day-to-day operations of the school district. The school budget is narrower in scope and covers the day-to-day operation of a specific school. While the school budget relies on gate receipts, resale items, fees, board of education revenue, state allocations, interest income, and fund-raising activities within the school for funding resources, the district budget relies on local taxes, state, and federal resources for funding its budget.

The framework for the school budget is found in board policy, and each school in the state of Tennessee must utilize the TAPM. The manual provides accountability, consistency, and efficiency for all Tennessee schools. The importance of this manual to the school principal cannot be overstated. All school boards of public education must adopt this manual and include the TAPM in its board policy. The inclusion of the TAPM ensures that the school principal must utilize the manual in the school's budgetary process of identifying revenue resources and accounting for the receiving and dispensing of school revenue. The TAPM clearly states the responsibilities of the principal and holds the school principal accountable for the day-to-day operation of the school and in implementing the rules and procedures for the school budget.

The school principal should adhere to the following steps in the budgeting process (Goldsmith, 2013):

1. Determine the allotment of revenue.
2. Identify fixed expenditures.
3. Involve all stakeholders.
4. Identify potential expenditures.
5. Develop a plan.
6. Set goals.
7. Utilize the TAPM for receiving and dispensing of revenue.
8. Abide by the budget.

To complete the budgetary process, the principal must present the school budget to the director of schools and board of education for approval.

Remember that the Tennessee school principal is responsible for the school budget and implementing the TAPM. Failure to adhere to this state and board policy directive may result in the removal of the principal.

CLASS ACTIVITIES

- Divide the class into PLCs and develop a school budget utilizing the forms found in the TAPM.
- Answer the following questions:

    1. Why was the TAPM adopted by Tennessee school boards?
    2. What is the TAPM?
    3. What are the sources of revenue of Tennessee schools? Explain how each source of revenue is obtained by the school.
    4. What are acceptable expenditures for the General Student Activity Fund?
    5. What are typical audit findings for Tennessee schools?

CHAPTER 8

FUNDING SOURCES FOR TENNESSEE SCHOOLS

Funding education adequately and equitably has always been a problem in America. As a direct result of inadequate and inequitable funding of schools, many lawsuits have erupted during the twentieth and twenty-first centuries against various state governments. Legal battles will probably continue throughout this century for adequate and equitable funding for public education.

A microscopic view of Tennessee's funding sources may be achieved by answering the following questions:

- What are the sources for funding education in Tennessee?
- What is the impact of taxes on educating the child with disabilities?
- What is a progressive and regressive tax?
- Does Tennessee have a fair tax system?

The purpose of this chapter is to answer these questions and to give the Tennessee administrator an expansive knowledge of Tennessee's tax structure. The increased understanding of Tennessee's tax structure should enable the Tennessee administrator to operate from the economic, political, and human resource frames in meeting the needs of the school and school district.

SOURCES OF TAX

The federal, state, and local governments collect taxes from four major tax silos: individual income, sales and gross receipts, corporation income, and property. However, the federal and state governments have access to many more types of taxes than local governments. For example, the federal government collects 81 percent of all individual income taxes, 81 percent of corporation taxes, and 23 percent of all sales excise taxes. In Tennessee, state government collects 63 percent of all sales and gross receipts taxes, and local government collects 100 percent of all property tax (Alexander and Salmon, 1995). The heavy use by the federal government of three of the four major types of tax is causing state and local governments to increase demands that the federal government return more of its revenue to them either directly, by a tax sharing plan, or by an increase of grants in aid.

Most Tennessee school districts depend on property tax for supporting education from the local government. Local option sales tax serves as the second major source of revenue. If the county's funding body votes to have a wheel tax referendum placed on the next election ballot, a wheel tax may serve as the third source of major revenue for education. A minor source of education revenue is derived from licenses, permits, beer, and liquor sales.

Special school districts in Tennessee request that the Tennessee legislature levy a tax for their school district. When the county assessor of property certifies to the appropriate county trustee the total assessed value of taxable property within the jurisdiction of the special school district, the school board reviews the certification. If additional revenue is required by the special school district, the board of education for the special school district shall vote in an announced meeting to exceed the certified rate as determined by the county tax assessor of property in the manner required of cities and counties and publish its intent. After publication of the board of education's intent, the board of education shall request legislation to exceed the certified rate (Tennessee, 2014).

Taxing authority must be derived from state constitutions or statutes. When collecting taxes, the Quid Pro Rational, the taxpayer should receive a benefit commensurate with the value of the tax. School taxes are state taxes, even though they may be levied at the local level. School districts cannot levy tax unless the power is conferred by statute.

TAXATION FOR PUBLIC SCHOOLS

There are two groups of taxes:

1. Taxes levied on the flow of production that are derived from purchases (sales tax)
2. Taxes on stock and wealth (property tax)

The first group of taxes focuses on sales taxes. In Tennessee, state government and local government utilize the sales tax to fund education. The state of Tennessee utilizes sales tax as the its base for operating state government with the largest percentage of sales tax revenue used for funding the Basic Education Program. While local governments use sale tax to moderately fund the operation of county and city services, that includes education.

The second group of taxes are levied on stock and wealth. Although Tennessee does not tax property, the state does have a Hall income tax. The Hall income tax is a personal income tax. The tax was levied on individuals, whose investments in stock, notes, and bonds yield earnings above $3,000,000. The Hall income tax is imposed only on individuals and other entities receiving interest from bonds, notes, and dividends from stock. It was enacted in 1929 and was originally called the Hall income tax for the senator who sponsored the legislation. Beginning January 1, 2017, House Bill 534/ Senate Bill 1221 reduces the Hall income tax rate by 1 percent each tax year with the year beginning January 1, 2018. The Hall income tax is fully repealed for tax years beginning January 1, 2021.

Local governments in Tennessee do tax personal wealth. The largest tax levied by local government is the property tax. School funding is based primarily on the property tax levy. The county assessor of property appraises property for assessment purposes and assess tax on tangible personal property used or held for use in business. The county commission and city governing bodies determine local property tax rates. The property tax is collected by county trustees and city collecting officials. Residential and farm property is taxed at 25 percent of its appraised value, and commercial and industrial property is taxed at 40 percent of its appraised value.

CONCLUSION

Equalized funding for public schools continues to be an issue in Tennessee. In 2004, Tennessee's Supreme Court found the state's education funding scheme unconstitutional for the third time, focusing specifically on teachers' salaries. In answer to the court's decision, Governor Bredesen appointed a task force on teacher pay, which recommended changing to a system-level fiscal capacity model for equalization, and the Tennessee General Assembly asked the Basic Education Program Review Committee that is appointed by the Tennessee State Board of Education to consider developing and implementing a system-level fiscal capacity model (Chervin, 2006).

A 2020 lawsuit charging that Tennessee underfunds its schools by hundreds of millions of dollars has been set for trial later this year. The litigation comes from Tennessee's largest school districts (Shelby County Schools and Metropolitan Nashville Public Schools). This lawsuit addresses adequacy, not equity. Previous lawsuits in Tennessee have focused on equity, and the Tennessee School Systems for Equity have prevailed in all three lawsuits.

In the September 2020, *Education Week* did an analysis of state spending and equity. Tennessee was given a D+ for school finance, and New Jersey was awarded an A–. The same study reveals that New Jersey was given a B for student achievement (K–12). Whereas, Tennessee was assessed a C– for student achievement (K–12) (Chen, 2020). A comparison of the two states is striking in that New Jersey has the largest per pupil expenditure, and Tennessee is ranked toward the bottom in school finance and average in student achievement. A quick observation by the reader reveals that a correlation seems to exist between student achievement and the financing of public education in Tennessee.

Why isn't Tennessee closing the student gap? Thirty-eight of 50 states are ahead of Tennessee in closing the student achievement gap (Chen, 2020). Many reasons have been given over the last two decades for Tennessee's rank in closing the student achievement gap. The chief reason has been the lack of money to achieve equity in Tennessee's school districts.

The state has given an enormous amount of money to school districts to improve student achievement and to achieve equity. However, *Education Week* (Chen, 2020) indicates that Tennessee has a laborious task ahead to rank in the top tier of states that are closing the student achievement gap in an equitable and adequate environment for all students in K–12.

State and local governments of Tennessee desire to provide a quality education for the 900,000 + students that are enrolled in public education. However, the tax structure of Tennessee is regressive and a political nightmare for state government, local government, school boards, and educational stakeholders. With property tax and the sales tax on goods as the base for obtaining the majority of revenue for education, one must expect political chaos with legislators, county commissioners, and members of the city council with the fear of not being reelected. Most of the elected officials seek office on the political platform of reducing or not raising taxes.

Tax is nothing but a mandatory contribution, levied by the government, without reference to any benefit to the taxpayer, in return for the tax paid. Taxes are classified as a progressive tax and a regressive tax. A progressive tax refers to the tax that rises with the rise in income. Conversely, the regressive tax is one wherein the rate of tax decreases with the increase in the taxable amount and taxes one-tenth of the wealth of the poor (Surbhi, 2016).

A progressive tax is an assessment on income or profit and is based on the ability to pay. A personal income tax that is levied by the state would benefit the low-income or poor taxpayer. For example, if a person did not earn profit or wages of at least $20,000 a year, he/she would be exempt from a personal income tax. As an added bonus for the taxpayer who does have to pay a state income tax, the amount paid to the state for income tax is deductible from the tax owed to the federal government.

A regressive tax is an assessment based on the percentage of an asset that is purchased. A sales tax and property tax are examples of a regressive tax, and everyone pays this tax. The regressive tax is a tax that is collected from low-income, middle-income, and high-income earners. A regressive tax does not consider the taxpayers level of income. One is easily able to understand that the high-income group of taxpayers profit from this tax.

Tennessee's tax system structure is built on a regressive tax. The regressive tax is a burden to the poor. All high-income taxpayers profit from the utilization of the sales and property tax. Operating in the political frame, the agenda for the person running for state or public office is to not "raise taxes." As a result, the state is reluctant to raise sales tax to fund education, and the local governing body is reluctant to raise property tax.

State government will fund roads with a regressive tax on gasoline and nobody complains, and local government will raise the property tax for the fire, police, and emergency services without a harsh voter response. On the other hand, state statute prevents the gasoline tax levied by the state from being used for other purposes, except for the repair and building new roads, and local governments use property tax to fund the aforementioned services for the safety and protection of its citizens. The quality of education suffers, and the "losers" are the children and stakeholders of public education.

There should be no "losers" in education, only "winners." If one truly believes in providing a quality and equitable education for the students of Tennessee, the regressive tax system of Tennessee must be reformed.

CLASS ACTIVITIES

- Divide the class into Professional Learning Communities (PLCs). Each PLC shall select a topic that is associated with the Tennessee tax system. The topic must be approved by the professor, and each PLC will utilize a PowerPoint presentation to show the results of their research.
- Identify and explain the sources of tax in Tennessee.
- Define the following terms:
    1. Sales tax
    2. Regressive tax
    3. Property tax
    4. Progressive tax
    5. Income tax
    6. In lieu of taxes
    7. Mill
    8. Ad valorem
- What is your opinion of the Tennessee Tax System for funding education?

ABOUT THE AUTHOR

Dr. Keith D. Brewer has had a successful career as a leader in the field of education for the state of Tennessee. Born and raised in Grundy County, he excelled in school and graduated high school as valedictorian. He finished his Bachelor of Science degree in Agricultural Education from the University of Tennessee in Knoxville in 1972. In 1979, Brewer completed his Master of Education Administration and Supervision degree from the University of Tennessee in Chattanooga. He earned his doctorate degree in School Leadership from Vanderbilt University in 1990.

Dr. Brewer has served in numerous educational positions throughout his career including: teacher, principal, Director of Schools, Director of a Regional Office for the State Department of Education, Deputy Commissioner of Education for Governor Phil Bredesen, Executive Director for the Tennessee Organization of School Superintendents, and adjunct professor. He currently serves as an educational consultant.

Dr. Brewer and his wife, Anita, have been married since 1982. They have three children and five grandchildren. He has devoted his career to teaching and influencing students, teachers, administrators, and educational leaders across Tennessee.

keithdbrewer.com

REFERENCES

Alexander, K., & Salmon R. G. (1995). Public school finance. Needham Heights: Allyn & Bacon.

Alexander, K., Salmon, R. G., & Alexander, F. K. (2015). Financing public schools. New York: Routledge.

Bedenbaugh, E. H. (1985). Education is still a good investment. The Clearing House, 59 *(3)*, 134–136.

Brewer, A. K. (2020, April). Unstructured interview with Retired Special Education and ESEA Director.

Brimley, V., & Burrup, P. (1982). Education in a climate of change (3rd. ed.). Boston: Allyn & Bacon, Inc.

Brown, P. R., & Elmore, R. F. (1982). Analyzing the impact of school finance reform. In N. H. Cambron-McCabe & A. Odden (Eds.), The changing of politics of school finance (pp. 107-138). Cambridge: Ballinger Publishing Company.

Burnette, D. (2019, February 12). Which states are poised to tackle outdated K-12 funding formulas? *Education Week*, pp. 1-5.

Burrup, P., Brimley, V., & Garfield, R. (1988). Financing education in a climate of change (4th ed.). Boston: Allyn & Bacon, Inc.

Chen, S. C. (2020, September 2). Quality counts 2020 grading the states. *Education Week*, p. 13.

Chervin, H. A. (2006). Searching for a fiscal capacity model.. Nashville: Tennessee Advisory Commission on Intergovernmental Relations.

Cohn, E. (1974). Economics of state aid to education. Toronto: D. C. Heath & Company.

Connelly, M. J., & McGee, J. (1987). School finance litigation of the 1980's. Journal of Education Finance, 12, 578-591.

Cubberly, E. (1905). School funds and their appportionment. New York: Columbia University.

Education Week (2007). "How *Education Week* Graded the States".

Education Week (2019). "The Affect That the Economy Has on American Education".

Ellerson, N. (2019). *American Association of School Administrators*. Retrieved from www.aasa.org/uploadedFiles/Policy_and_Advocacy/IDEA-FF-Fact-Sheet.pdf http://www.aasa.org

Every Student Succeeds Act, Pub. L114-9820 U.S.C. CH. 28 (2015).

Finance, T. D.-O. (2011). *Tennessee Internal School Uniform Accounting Policy.* (T. Comptroller, Ed.) Nashville, Tennessee, United States: State of Tennessee.

Geske, T. G., & Zuelke, D. C. (1982). Cost-effectiveness Analyses: A Practical Tool for Educational Planning and Changing. Planning and Changing, 13 (1), 3-10.

Gibbs, J. (1979). Tennessee School Finance Equity Study. Proceedings of the Superintendents' Study Council.

Goldsmith, R. D. (2013). The principal's guide to school budgeting (2nd ed.). Thousand Oaks: Corwin.

Hancock, M. (2019). *Understanding Special Education Funding.* Retrieved from UnderstandingSpecialEducation.com: https://www.understandingspecialeducation.com/special-education-law.html.

Hickrod, G. & Chaudhari, R. (1972). National Conference on School Finance. Washington, DC: National Education Association.

Huss, D. C. (2009). School Finance with Related School Law. Unpublished manuscript.

Johns, R. L., Morphet, E. L., & Alexander, K. (1983). The economics and financing of education. Englewood Cliffs, NJ: Prentice Hall, Inc.

Johns, R. L., Morphet, E. L. & Stollar, D. H. (1971). Status and Impact of Educational and Finance Programs. National Education. Finance Project.

Legislature, T. (2013). *Tennessee Code Annotated Title67, Chapter 2.* Charlottesville: Matthew Bender & Company, Inc.

McLaughlin, M. W., & Catterall, J. S. (1984). Notes on the new politics of education. Education and Urban Society, 16 (3), 375-381.

Mort, P. R. (1933). State Support for Public Education. Washington, DC: United States Office for Public Education.

National Center for Education Statistics (2010).

Newman, J. (1990, May 1990). Give school boards taxing authority: Counsultant. Tennessee Town and City. p.1.

Norlin, J. W. (2009). The answer book on special education law. (vol. 2 5th ed.). Horsham: LRP Publications.

Odden, A. (1983, January). School finance reform in the states: 1983. Phi Delta Kappan, pp. 5-40.

Peevely, G. L. (1980). The measurement of equity in tennessee school finance. Unpublished doctoral dissertation, University of Tennessee, Knoxville, Tennessee.

Robinson v. Cahill 303 A. 2d 273 (N.J. 1973).

Surbhi, S. (2016, July 5). *Difference Between Progressive and Regressive Tax.* Retrieved from Key Differences: http://

www.keydifferences.com/difference-between-progressive-regressivetax.html.

Shockley, G. D. (1989). School administrator's budget handbook. Englewood Cliffs, NJ: Prentice Hall.

Sparkman, W. E. (1983). School Finance litigation in the 1980's. In S. B. Thomas, N. H. Cambron-McCabe, & M. M. McCarth (Eds.), Educators and the law: Current trends and issues (pp. 96-108). Boston: Allyn & Bacon, Inc.

Strayer, G. D. (1923). The Financing of Education in the State of New York. New York: MacMillian Company.

Tennessee, State o. (2014). TN Code 67-5-1704. Nashville, Tennessee, United States.

US Department of Education (2015). Public Law 114-95.

Wright, D. S. (2020, March). Unstructured interview with Assistant Professor at Lincoln Memorial University.

Made in the USA
Monee, IL
08 April 2025

15412164R00089